TROPICAL FLOWERS

Dr. Hans W. Hannau

STORY BY JEANNE GARRARD

DOUBLEDAY & COMPANY INC.
GARDEN CITY, NEW YORK

Cover design by Bill Hays

To a gifted flower designer and dear friend
Jenny Schroeder,
who inspired this book

Hans W. Hannau

ISBN:0-385-03993-X
Library of Congress Catalog Card Number 73-81519
All rights reserved by the author.
Composed in the United States.
Printed in Spain.

CONTENTS

INTRODUCTION 9

WHERE DID TROPICAL FLOWERS ORIGINATE? 10

HAWAII—THE FLOWER ISLANDS 10

AMERICAS' SUBTROPICAL ZONE 11

TROPICAL AMERICAS AND WEST INDIES 13

CANARY ISLANDS, MADEIRA ISLANDS, THE AZORES 14

TROPICAL AFRICA 15

ASIA: EAST PAKISTAN, INDIA, CHINA, INDONESIA,
THAILAND, JAVA, SUMATRA, MALAYAN PENINSULA 40

AUSTRALIA 41

THE PHILIPPINES 43

PLANT HUNTERS 44

FAMILIES OF TROPICAL FLOWERS 71

FAVORITE TROPICAL FLOWERS 76
    ORCHIDS 76
    BROMELIADS 78
    CACTI AND SUCCULENTS 79
    ANTHURIUMS 104
    GINGER 105

BOTANICAL GARDENS 107

TROPICAL FLOWERS IN HOME AND GARDEN 112

THE COLOR PICTURES

VANDA ORCHID 17
VANDA ORCHID HYBRID 18
CATTLEYA HYBRID 19
CATTLEYA PERCIVALIANA 19
RENANTHERA ORCHID 20
CYMBIDIUM ORCHID 20
DORITAENOPSIS ORCHID 21
PHALAENOPSIS ORCHID 21
GUZMANIA (Bromeliad) 22
BILLBERGIA (Bromeliad) 22
FOSTERIANA (Bromeliad) 23
WATER HYACINTH 24
TROPICAL WATER LILIES 25
BIRD OF PARADISE 26
TORCH GINGER 27
FIRE GINGER 27
AFRICAN VIOLETS 28
GLOXINIAS 29
FIG MARIGOLD 30
ICE PLANT 30
HELICONIA 31
PROTEA 32
AFRICAN TULIP TREE 49
FRANGIPANI 50
CHORISIA 51
GOLDEN SHOWER 52
ROYAL POINCIANA 53
SAGO PALM 54
CHACONIA 55
DWARF POINCIANA 55
HIBISCUS 56

CRAPE MYRTLE...57
PINK POUI TREE..58
GOLD TREE..59
ORCHID TREE..59
BOTTLE BRUSH TREE..60
CANDLEBUSH in BLOOM..60
CHENILLE PLANT..61
BOMBAX BLOOM..61
MORNING GLORY...62
POTATO BUSH...62
POINSETTIA..63
BANANA BLOSSOM..64
FLAME VINE...81
ALLAMANDA..82
SKY VINE..83
BLUE PASSION FLOWER..84
PURPLE GRANADILLA..84
GIANT GRANADILLA..85
SCARLET PASSION FLOWER..85
BOUGAINVILLEA...86
BOUGAINVILLEA SUNGLOW...87
CORAL VINE..88
PETREA...89
IXORA..90
ANTHURIUM...90
SHRIMP PLANT...91
PELICAN FLOWER..91
TROPICAL FLOWER ARRANGEMENTS....................................92, 93
MONSTERA DELICIOSA..94
QUEEN OF THE NIGHT...95
ANGELS TRUMPET...96

INTRODUCTION

God must have created tropical flowers from warm glows lighting His heart or twinkles in His eyes ... for these same emotions stir humankind at each glimpse.

Analytical scientists say, literally, tropical flora should be born and live within terrestrial belts parallel to the equator, bound by celestial Tropics of Cancer and Capricorn at 23°27′ north and south. Since these tropics spawn diverse climatic ranges, by altitude, from humid jungles to snow-capped peaks, semantic and horticultural values clash.

Plantsmen use "tropical" to designate flower characteristcs and requirements of warmth-loving plants of lower altitudes in both the tropics and sub-tropics. *(Exotica* has limits of these marked on a world map.) Tropical flowers, thus, are discovered growing outdoors in warm climates or in planned environments indoors such as those provided in botanical gardens, office buildings and private homes.

Synergetic symbiosis — or at least intimate cooperation — between plants and humankind, shuffled distribution and improved hybrids by natural selection of original flowers so greatly that arguments arise, even today, over origins or native ownership.

WHERE DID TROPICAL FLOWERS ORIGINATE?

Origins possess importance, but, in themselves, do not predict where the most beautiful tropical flowers can be seen today — whether in tropical and subtropical areas . . . northern or foreign conservatories . . . botanical gardens.

Humankind-guardians, coupled with nature's whims and peoples' desires, frequently dictate. They create gardens where none existed . . . encourage natural proliferation . . . finance advancement.

Economics commissioned early plant expeditions only for utilitarian products. Fortunately, God instilled insatiable curiosity plus aesthetics in most plantsmen and botanists so they sneaked in a few purely decorative flowering plants before most men were willing to pay for it.

Immigrant plants enrich their new homelands. Consider these peculiarities: a bulb secretly "spirited" out of Turkey made Holland famous for Tulips; an Egyptian plant, Coffee, made Brazil rich; Chocolate, a Brazilian native, grows best in Liberia; Brazil's native Rubber succeeds better in Malaya; South America isn't famous for Pineapples which originated there — Hawaii is!

HAWAII — THE FLOWER ISLANDS

HAWAII — Dream Flower Islands of the Pacific — owes outsiders . . . of other lands and people . . . for almost all its present floral splendor.

Golden-tanned Hawaiian girls greet travelers today with lei garlands of fragrant Frangipanis, Vanda Orchids or rainbows of Hibiscus — few of which are truly native. Frangipanis originated in the West Indies and South America; Vandas from Southeast Asia (India to New Guinea); Hibiscus mostly from Asia and East Africa. Only two in the Hibiscus family — whose names are rarely known by the viewing public — Ilima and Mahoe, are considered to have originated on these islands. Yet Hawaii never disappoints flower-loving visitors.

Exotics such as the Bird-of-Paradise, Flamingo Flower Anthuriums, Orchids, Flaming Gingers, are commercially exported today — some, even back to their homelands.

Interrelating with flowers and nature so much, people of the Hawaiian Islands instilled love of flowers into visitors and native born. Island scientists improved species, sought new hybrids and better techniques in mass-growing until Hawaii's floral reputation lured the world to its shores.

"Liquid sunshine" — according to Hawaiians — is the natural secret of what creates their luxuriant vegetation plus clean healthful climate. This misty spray freshens the environment at least once a day. Its feathery touch bedews, invigorates without chilling. It nurtures all life.

Invasion of the Hawaiian Islands — by hordes of welcome visitors and "introduced" ornamental plants — has so dangerously threatened endemic flora with rapid extinction that protective national parks have been established. The best known is Haleakala with its volcanic moonscape and remote dinosaur-like vegetation. Since this strange growth evolved in island-isolation, along with other unusual flora, it can be found nowhere else on earth. But perhaps Hawaiian floral-friendliness or less remote flowers — even in promotional/commercial zeal — does more to spread love and information about tropical flowers.

AMERICAS' SUBTROPICAL ZONE

FLORIDA — sister "Land of Flowers" — like Hawaii, has developed similarly. Many of its flowers and people were originally visitors who became contented residents . . . immigrants — naturalized.

Myriads of unique and beautiful flowers burst into bloom every day of the year. Rare plant materials — especially in South Florida — are bewildering horticultural mixtures of natives intermingled with international tropical species. In extremely few other places — even deep tropics — can more kinds of ornamental plants be found growing naturally today. These advantages — plus world recognition and an international visitor-flow — make Florida a showcase of tropical flowers plus their transition. This showcase demonstrates the rest of the world's — as well as North America's — Subtropical flower potentials.

The best of at least three horticultural and floral zones are available within its shores, but only Florida's southern three-quarters are actually subtropical . . . where tropical flowers are happy outdoors.

Bordering on the true Tropics, Subtropical climatic natural environments are an extension of the Tropics. This extended area fans out into places that often have lower temperature spells in winter, but rarely and of short duration. Florida's Sun-tropical temperatures seem to flow up to softly rolling hills and a network of spring-fed lakes just past the center of the state with warmer temperatures easing on up the coastlines. Hardier tropical and subtropical flowers bloom as far north as Jacksonville while "tender" exotics flourish only in warmer gardens near coast lines or further south.

Tropical flowers bloom anytime they wish — even at night — in Subtropical Florida where Spring and warmth radiate perpetually.

Botanical gardens of the world inspire tourist attractions, which often can lavish more money and efforts on massive displays of flowers. (Botanists realize they reach diverse segments of the population rarely seen in Botanical greenhouses.) Like Botanical Gardens with greenhouses, many Attractions try to design, duplicate and compress spectacular sights the average person could not manage to see — at least without great expense, greater interest and hardship. Florida gardens can symbolize all areas developed by plant-lovers interested in promoting tourists as well as flower growing and tropical flower research.

SISTER-STATES in climate form North America's only other Subtropical areas famous for flowers such as California Golden Poppy and Texas Blue Bonnet. Adaptable tropical flowers grow in Lower California, Baja California, the southern tip of Texas, land fringes of states bordering the Gulf of Mexico with small forests, jungles, swamps or bayous, and lowlands of northern Mexico.

SUBTROPICAL SOUTH AMERICA is almost the same in climatic floral benefits extending to southern Chile and Bahia Blanca, Argentina.

Petunias — relatively latecomers to botanical history — were discovered growing just a little north, near the Rio de la Plata, in 1823 by French explorers and sent to French Botantist Jussieu.

Zinnias — from a little further north, in Brazil — reached Europe over half a century before Petunias but both took time to adjust to garden life elsewhere and become popular annuals. Today a hundred varieties of Zinnias are available, from pigmy size with quarter or shilling-size blooms to giant plants producing flowers eight inches across.

MEXICO — land of historical flower lovers — is famous for contributing two outstanding flowers, Dahlias and that floral symbol of Christmas — Poinsettias, *Euphorbia pulcherrima*. The Poinsettia family is an old one scattered over the world. A smaller cousin, Annual Poinsettia, is almost as brilliant and grows wild on north into the United States. (Chaconia, Wild Poinsettia of Trinidad is magnificent but not related.) Mexico's Crimson Bell or Coral Bell Heucheras traveled too but Dahlias won greater human support.

Aztecs — Mexico's early empire-builders — were architects and garden builders, like early Egyptians. Both empires were conquered. Their cities and gardens crumbled into ruins but both civilizations left records. These records endured and so did their cultivated flowers. Our garden Dahlias were originally grown for food from their tubers as well as for flowers. The Aztec Indians developed a double Dahlia also. Since their empire extended through Central America on into South America, these Mexicans grew and improved many plants credited to other countries. For instance, Nasturtiums are credited as originating through Spanish conquest in South America, as are Tobacco (often credited only to North American Indians) and Sunflowers. History records that Sunflowers were used in Aztec religious ceremonies in Mexico as well as Peru. Yet when the Sunflower came to Europe in Elizabeth's reign, it was titled by English Herbalist Gerard, the "Golden Flower of Peru." He said this flower ". . . in one summer . . . hath risen up to the height of fourteen foot in my garden . . .". Today the Sunflower is more commercially grown for oil and seed-cake than as a garden annual.

Fascinating avenues of history and exploration cloud origins of a few flowers — or make them "borderline" tropical flowers which may or may not have first bloomed in the "true Tropics."

TROPICAL AMERICAS AND WEST INDIES

Flamboyant flowers flaunting their vivid reds and yellows or amazing viewers with their bizarre shapes and scents, generally came from the "true Tropics" — those lands within the Tropics of Cancer and Capricorn — centering the world. Today they are cultivated outdoors in warmer climates and indoors in colder areas all over the world.

Rarity plus tales of adventure enhance — thus showy blossoms from jungles or islands-in-the-sun excite gardeners from colder climates.

Snow-capped peaks may be less than 20,000 foot-steps away from the warmest temperatures in sea-level jungles. Climates vary greatly depending on altitudes within tropical zones . . . so do flowers.

Orchids, Bird-of-Paradise, Ginger, Royal Poincianas, Flamingo Flowers, Night-Blooming Cereus, Bromeliads, Passion Flowers, Golden Showers, and Water Lilies spring to mind with thoughts of tropic lands whether in Eastern or Western Hemispheres. Both regions — Old World tropics and New World tropics — still contain hidden floral treasures in as yet unexplored areas awaiting their world debuts into garden society of the "select 500."

Selecting 500 exotic plants, then researching their origins reveals that more of today's favorites come from the Tropical Americas (including West Indies.) East Indies, Malaya, China, India, Burma, South Africa and Madagascar — all lumped together — can produce a close "second" quantity out of this 500-tropical-origin collection. But Western Tropics will hold their lead.

"Nowhere is there as great a variety," says Alfred B. Graf in his *Exotica,* "nor such a wealth of endemic plant types as in Tropical America." He is speaking not only about tropical flowers but also of thousands of delightful houseplants grown more for their beauty in foliage coloration or striking design in foliage rather than flowers. These would include Ferns, Crotons, Fancy-Leaved Caladiums, Cacti, Palms, Coleus, Alocasias, Peperomias, Rex Begonias, Marantas, Diffenbachias and Dracaenas — certainly considered tropical as well as beautiful even though their flowers aren't showy.

CANARY ISLANDS, MADEIRA ISLANDS, THE AZORES

CANARY ISLANDS — even the name wings into space — suggesting songs and flowers. Teneriffe, largest island of the Canaries, is known as "Island of Eternal Peace" and "Island of Flowers" drawing visitors to its shores for equitable climates, magnificent beaches and floral splendor. This splendor must be credited both to happy migrants as well as natives.

Floral gifts to the world from the Canaries are rare native treasures from varied altitudes. For instance, the Teide-violet with its amethyst-blue and yellow striped flower, springs from frosty-soil and pumice stone crags of Pico de Teide while heat-loving Canary Date Palms live at low altitudes over the islands but came from silent glens (barrancos) on Teneriffe.

Mysterious and most famous of native flora is the Canarian Dragon Tree *(Dracaena draco)* with its odd "60-million-year-old" shape and reddish resin once believed possessed of mystic powers when it turned into "dragon's blood." Most striking of the 450 endemic species is *Euphorbia canariensis* with red flowers popping from sparse limbs on moisture-holding pillar-like trunk. Other interesting natives include Green Rosebuds of genus Grennovia succulents, *Chrysanthemum frutescens* and the Red Cistus. About 1,100 migrant flowering species have found a "home away from home" in the middle of the Atlantic on the warm Canaries about 218 miles west of Africa. Some such as Bougainvillaeas, Daturas, Hibiscus, yellow-lined white Frangipanis and African Tulip Trees flower beautifully here as do introduced tropical fruit trees. A little higher up, native Campanula and Digitalis species are abundant. Teneriffe has only 782 square miles but a variety of altitudes up to 12,190 feet above the warm Canary Current in the sea, so a splendid variety of flowers can be seen within a few miles of all their tropical flowers.

PORTUGUESE ARCHIPELAGO — The Azores in the Atlantic southwest of Lisbon — is noted for gorgeous unspoiled semi-tropical scenery and quaint old customs. The Azores and Madeira Islands, southwest of Portugal, show a gathering of flowers from all parts of the world. Because Portuguese were such early and master sailors, they helped spread flowers to various ports and brought their favorites home to these islands. Madeira is popularly known for its wines and embroideries but botanists love its native *Gummy Aeonium* with foot-square flower clusters.

14

TROPICAL AFRICA

MADAGASCAR — mysterious plant world — gave beauties to the outer world. "A secluded shrine," said a 19th Century French scientist trying to describe Madagascar, "into which nature retreated to work on designs she does not employ anywhere else." Even today plants live there which defy origin ...relative or plant-order detection. Although only the 218 mile Mozambique Channel separates it from Africa, only a few plants and animals are common to both. Today about 75 percent of the original vegetation in three fourths of the island has been burned out by residents. Yet this island has bequeathed a treasure of tropical flowers to the world ... abundant, fragrant and waxy Bridal Bouquet *(Stephanotis floribunda)* vine, lavender-pink flowered Madagascar Rubber vine; perennial pink and white Periwinkle *(Catharanthus roseus);* Butterfly Bush Buddleias; Pink Ball Dombeya hybrids; orange Colville's Glory and that glorious Royal Poinciana *(Delonix regia)* whose famed scarlet or yellow-red "Umbrella-shaped" trees are so admired they are grown around the world; a famous Shooting Star Orchid with a 12-inch tail, *Angraecum sesquipedale,* was found there as was Travelers' Palm Ravenalas, "Old World" Cacti, Alluaudia and Didiera; and the "Mother" of Giant Baobabs, *Adamsonia grandidieri,* which at 131 feet tall and elephantine trunks dwarfs the famous African species *(A. digitata)* and is one of the many biological oddities on this island. Baobabs are thought to reach the age of 2,500 years and be among oldest living things on earth.

AFRICA — Oddities were often the first plant treasures out of a region. When early sailing ships rounded the cape of South Africa and put in for supplies or rest, travelers saw flora completely alien to their eyes. So April Fool *(Haemanthus rotundifolius)* and leafless hairy-blossomed Carrion Flowers fascinated everyone. They were first pictured in early botanical drawings and taken to Europe along with the lovely Proteas and Heaths.

First African Cape flower drawn was in 1605, pictured in Clusius' *Exoticum libridecem* and Clusius likened its flower head to a thistle — about 100 years later the name changed to Protea. Africa has 400 species and 14 Protea genera, only exceeded by 750 Australian species ... but the showiest King Protea comes from South Africa. On a five or six foot bush, this King Protea often has "exploding-star-petals-upon-petals" flower-heads up to 12 inches across (actually hundreds of flowers held by colorful bracts) called "honey pots," for their nectar.

Tropical African flowers — Orchids, for instance, are still being discovered

(Continued on page 39)

Descriptions of the following pictures

Page 17

Vanda Orchid *(Vanda tricolor)*

This Vanda is fragrant but rarely used for corsages for its petals have a 180 degree twist. Blooms are highly variable in coloration and shape but all densely red-brown dotted and 2 to 3 inches wide. Originally from range of India to New Guinea, Vandas and their hybrids are cultivated world wide today.

Page 18

Vanda Orchid Hybrid (V. Josephine van Brero X V. Marelmae Kamanele)

Unusual color, from these delicate orange and peach combinations to brown variations and even to blues, makes Vanda hybrids choice flowers for corsages, arrangements and specimen plants. Semi-terete Vandas such as this will bloom when a small plant but since the plant continues to grow to a sizeable form, many hobby growers find their space too limited to include these plants even though their blossoms are distinctive and long-lasting. For hobbyists in tropical or subtropical climates, these orchids make fine yard plants and they are seen outdoors in large numbers. Children are also fascinated with the "monkey" that sits in the center of most of these blooms. Originally from southeastern Asia, they are grown all over the world especially in tropical and sub-tropical zones.

Page 19 (top)

Cattleya Orchid Hybrid

Vibrant color, "golden eyes" and deeper fringed lip make this pair of Cattleya flowers lovely to wear as corsages or to keep on the potted plant for long-lasting home decoration. Cattleyas have long been considered the "Queen" of Orchids and rich "royal" colors help create that image even more. Cattleyas from Tropical America have been the most popular for hybridizing.

Page 19

Cattleya Percivaliana Variety Grandiflora 'Sonia'

Cattleya Percivaliana *variety grandiflora 'Sonia' is an especially fine species plant from Venezuela showing more shape than many hybrids. It usually flowers in winter around Christmas or later with 4 to 5 inch flowers with deep orange or deep golden throats.* C. Percivalianas *are usually lavender with golden throats but this is a rarer white.*

(Continued on page 33)

VANDA ORCHID HYBRID

ORCHIDS

For detailed description see page 16

CATTLEYA
ORCHID
HYBRID

CATTLEYA
ORCHID

19

RENANTHERA
ORCHID SPRAY

For detailed description see page 33

CYMBIDIUM
ORCHID HYBRID

20

SPRAY ORCHID, DORITAENOPSIS

MOTH ORCHID, PHALAENOPSIS

21

← *BROMELIAD THORCH, GUZMANIA*

BILLBERGIA FOSTERIANA →

BROMELIADS

BILLBERGIA PYRAMIDALIS

WATER HYACINTH

For detailed description see page 35

TROPICAL
WATER LILIES

GOLDEN WATER LILY

BIRD OF PARADISE, STRELITZIA REGINAE

TORCH GINGER

For detailed description see page 36

AFRICAN VIOLETS

For detailed description see page 37

GLOXINIAS

SINNINGIA SPECIOSA

FIG MARIGOLD

MESEMBRYANTHEMUM

ICE PLANT

LOBSTER CLAW, HELICONIA

For detailed description see page 38

(Continued from page 16)

Descriptions of the foregoing pictures

Page 20

Red Orchid Spray *(Renanthera Brookie Chandler)*

Fire red sprays of orchids on this Renanthera hybrid orchid spice up the luxurious green area around the lily pool in the Rare Plant House at Fairchild Tropical Garden. Renanthera is from the Greek for kidney-shaped and another or pollen-bearing part of a stamen (which in orchids is joined with pistil into a single organ called a column). Renanthera are normally tree-perching or epiphytic but can be grown in pots. These are Indo-Malayan orchids rarely grown by hobbyists in other parts of the United States because of the size of the plant. There is a Renanthera (R. imschootiana) *often found in small greenhouse collections with red and yellow flowers nearly 2 inches wide growing on a plant only about 12 inches tall. Other blooms in this picture are coming up from a Cow's Horn Orchid* (Cyrtopodium punctatum).

Page 20

Cymbidium Orchid Hybrid

There are about 50 species and untold numbers of hybrids of Cymbidium orchids. They originated in the Old World Tropics, many from Burma, but have been hybridized and loved for over 30 years. In some areas of the United States, where they can have "warm heads and cool feet" or sun on foliage and cool water for roots, these are grown as garden plants but are actually epiphytes. The name Cymbidium is Greek for boat in allusion to the lip shape but this reasoning seems to escape most people. Flowers are extremely showy in arching clusters that are very long lasting — thus their popularity as corsage flowers and house plants. Waxy colors are unlike other delicate orchid shades.

Page 21 (top)

Spray Orchids, Moth Orchids *(Doritaenopsis Dorette)*

Vibrantly colored Doritaenopsis Dorette has exceptionally long sprays of 2" flowers. These plants bloom profusely over an extended period making them popular for private and public conservatories all over the world. Doritaenopsis originated by a cross of Doritis with Phalaenopsis, closely allied genera, in Hawaii in 1923. Numerous different hybrids have been created since then but few surpass this beauty.

Page 21 (lower right)

Moth Orchid Spray *(Phalaenopsis Palmbel)*

One of the few orchids with lush pretty foliage but grown for its gracefully flowing sprays of white (also other colors) blossoms, Phalaenopsis orchids are without rival in the orchid world. Mostly native of Indo-Malayan region the finest species originally came from the Philippine Islands but hybridizing has grown in other areas of the world each year since these lovely orchids were introduced. Their long sprays move in the slightest breeze making their blossoms seem like moths on the wing. Flowers last on the plants for several months. This hybrid beauty was created in Florida.

Page 22 (top)

Bromeliad Torch *(Guzmania lingulata)*

Bromeliads are all striking plants or have wildly colorful designs in their inflorescences. They are becoming increasingly popular as hobbyists' pets and house plants being grown either for their showy "flowers" or handsome, often gaudily colored, foliage. Their flowers are borne in bright bracts which are often considered together as one large "flower". Like almost every Bromeliad, these fold the base of their leaves in a tight overlapping rosette forming a cup that holds water. Since each leaf forms a special gutter down to this reservoir, water is always available to the plant. Relatives of the Pineapple family, Bromeliads are from Tropical America and many of these are air-plants which you can see growing on trees.

Page 22 (lower)

Bromeliad, Pretty Pineapple, Air Plant *(Billbergia pyramidalis)*

This charming member of the Pineapple family spreads easily but retains individual broad-leafed open rosettes of green-gold shade. Its short erect flower spike builds up to a large compact head of radiant pink bracts and masses of pink flowers tipped in brilliant blue. Of the 40 genera and 1,000 species, many are grown on the ground or in trees. Bromeliads and pineapples are symbols of hospitality. When the Spanish fleet first visited the West Indies, they found that when pineapples or pineapple tops were placed near the entrance to a village or on the top of a hut, the Indians welcomed them as good friends.

Page 23

Bromeliad on Driftwood *(Billbergia Fosteriana)*

Bromeliads grow easily on driftwood to make a fascinating conversation piece for patio gardens. Their colorful inflorescences and intriguing variegated foliage add interest and design to any area whether in home or garden. Bromeliads attach easily and their roots take hold firmly in a short time. They are good companion plants for Orchids and Ferns creating a naturalistic setting. The picture shows Billbergia Fosteriana *from Brazil which is also often called* B. Fantasia.

Page 24

Water Hyacinth *(Eichhornia crassipes)*

"Gallant galleons with fragile lavender sails" is a poetic way of describing the Water Hyacinth. "Expensive pest that chokes otherwise navigable streams" is the more usual way it is described in southern U.S.A., Gulf States, Florida, and several tropical countries where Water Hyacinth population-explosion has reached uncontrollable proportions. Until you must battle them, these handsome floating aquatics look like a luxuriant green and violet carpet floating on streams and lakes. Flower spikes are profuse sticking up well above air-filled bulbs and green leaves showing upper flower lobes blue-patched and yellow dotted over the violet. It is well to remember the "beast" of overly abundant self-propagation in this "beauty" if you transplant it to new waters. Until then, you can enjoy a floating field of silken color on tropical waters. Various authorities say the Water Hyacinth originated in East Africa, South America and India as well as Florida, but history shows it was introduced into Florida and probably to other countries mentioned above.

Page 25 (Top)

Tropical Water Lilies *(Nymphaeaceae)*

Tropical Water Lilies originate chiefly in Africa and India and range in color from white to blues, dark reds and yellows. Only about 4 species and half dozen hybrids are readily available from nurseries. The Red Bengal Water Lily from India has many varieties and hybrids while the largest of all aquatic plants in the world is the Royal Water Lily with white flowers that turn rosy and saucer-like leaves up to 7 or 8 ft. wide. This and other fine ones are usually found in larger Botanical Gardens.

Page 25 (Lower)

Golden Water Lily *(Nymphaea St. Louis)*

A Golden Water Lily blooms in tropical early morning light. It is the first yellow flowering hybrid and usually shares the limelight with other colored blooms. These aquatic plants furnish showy flowers for people to admire plus shade and a place to hide for tropical fish and gold fish. Sometimes round floating leaves serve as rafts for colorful butterflies to rest on or as sun-porches for frogs and tiny birds.

Bird of Paradise, Queen's Flower, Blue Tongue Bird of Paradise (*Strelizia reginae*)

A provocative and challenging exotic bird-flower was first introduced from South Africa into England in the reign of George III and named after the Queen. Flowers are borne inside a pink or purplish-flushed sheath shaped like a bird's beak or a keel of a boat almost at right angles to the stem. Flowers spring out, usually one or two at a time, like the crest of a bird from its head or sails from a boat. Two brilliant orange (sometimes red) petaloid sepals pop out to stand upright flickering like flames. A third sepal lies flat until pushed up by the next opening flower. Petals are a deep blue with the stigma the javelin or arrow-like part of the flower. Usually tiny sun-birds pollinate the flowers. When they perch on the two lateral petals and depress them slightly, the anthers are sprung out of a tube and dust the bird's breast with pollen.

Page 27 (Top)

Fire Ginger, Red Ginger, Fiery Feather *(Alpinia purpurata)*

Large open-spaced rich crimson bracts as delicate as petals hide shy true flowers. This flaming spike stands erect and proud of its rosy-crimson beauty against dark green blade-shaped leaves. As the flower matures, it elongates and tiny green plantlets pop out between the bracts. As they grow and add weight to the feather end long stalk, the head bends over. Reaching ground, the plantlets take root and grow. Ginger comes in many other colors and shapes. It is originally from the South Pacific Islands.

Page 27 (Center)

Torch Ginger *(Nicolai elatior,* formerly *Phaeomeria magnifica*)

Famed Torch Gingers, by any name, are one of the most spectacular of tropical blooms. Its inflorescence tops a strong 3 to 5 foot stalk and looks like a large cone made up of fleshy but waxy red bracts. These red bracts fold back gracefully revealing tiny "true" flowers and the rounded cone-end of tightly overlapped bracts. Torch Gingers come from the East Indies originally where they grow in huge 18 to 20 foot clumps. There is also a radiant Pink Torch Ginger.

African Violets *(Saintpaulia ionantha)*

African Violets seem like old time favorites. Although discovered fairly late in the 19th century, this genus has become popular enough to have African Violet Societies in England and America. Originally native to tropical East Africa, their countless thousands of varieties and hybrids today offer immense color range plus single or double flowers. Typically violet blue, the flowers can be purple, red, blue, pink, white or combinations and hues of these. There are even rare varieties with orange and yellow flowers and true miniatures. Downy green leaves often display reddish glows beneath or may have a top "quilted" look. Flowers pop out fairly continuously and generously when healthy. When more than one crown develops in a pot, these plants tend to produce less flowers and more leaves.

Gloxinias *(Sinningia speciosa)*

Few flowers can beat Gloxinias in size, richness and variety of coloring. Their flowers are wide and tubular with fluted flaring petals which extend the open-bell to 5 or 6 inches in diameter. Some are intense colors of purple, red, blue, pink with white throats or some have their petals margined with a broad band of white or contrasting color. Some are dark spotted on white with a rich shade of fluting or ruffles with a yellow throat. Today's cultivated varieties and hybrids overshadow the original purple-flowered species found in Brazil. They can be raised from seed but bloom faster from older tubers which can be divided.

Fig Marigold *(Mesembryanthemum criniflorum)*, Sun Babies

"Sandgold," and "Cliff Saver" are names given to the strong growing, tough-trailing or creeping plants from Cape Province; South Africa. These Mesembryanthemum species are widely planted in California, Southern Europe and other coasts in sand or rocks to help control erosion on banks. Their flowers are about one inch across and they form a brilliant carpet which can even "drape" down over dunes and cliffs. Since these little beauties can grow in sand and tolerate salt spray, they are excellent seaside plants.

Page 30 (Lower)

Ice Plant *(Mesembryanthemum acinaciforme)*

These beauties are abundant on salt sprayed islands such as Bermuda. They are called purple Mesembs or Fig Marigolds along with other common names but this daisy-like genus has nearly 1,000 species known collectively as Mesembryanthema which has been split up into more than 100 genera in the Carpetweed Family (Aizoaceae). *Many originated in South Africa as succulent plants with trailing 3 angled stems and thick leaves to hold moisture and withstand heat.*

Page 31

Lobster Claw — Red Heliconia *(Heliconia sp.)*

Fantastic but real is this striking inflorescence of the Heliconia. All in this group, including the Lobster Claw and Hanging Heliconia, are remarkable sights which first-time viewers find hard to believe are real. Stiff brilliant boat-shaped bracts create the color and carry the inconspicuous true flowers. When Heliconias are not in bloom, they might easily be mistaken for a clump of Banana plants which are in the same family. These are sometimes called false Bird-of-Paradise. Species of Heliconias range in height from 2 to 12 feet tall but most are massive, needing room to spread by creeping rootstocks. Most are native to South and Central America.

Page 32

Protea *(Protea compacta)*

Protea blossoms are multi-petal-upon-petal unusual flower heads made up of colorful bracts around hundreds of flowers, that are often eight to twelve inches wide and have enough sweet nectar to make into sugar or local cough syrup. The Proteas come mostly from South Africa and Australia. Most are shrubs or small tree-like bushes with leathery leaves, some of which grow to 12 ft. The King Protea was one of the first and most spectacular flowers brought to England from South Africa. Colors of Proteas range from pinks to white, lavender-rose and red.

(Continued from page 15)

by the outside world and exported. Among them are Satyrium, Schizodium and *Disa uniflora*. The red *Disa uniflora,* a large flowering terrestrial orchid has become famous. It blooms about the same time as another red flower, *Rochea coccinea*. "Dark Continent" stories of vast unexplored areas are being "lighted" but all African regions still offer mystery and hidden treasures for botanists and especially for home gardeners in far off lands. New discoveries will pop up in nurseries of other lands for years to come.

In earlier days only the Cape Flora was known, with its small leathery-leaved plants and conspicuous flowers. Since Africa is so large, it has a great variety of flowering plants.

The most spectacular flower from Africa is the Bird-of-Paradise *(Strelitzia reginae)* of South Africa. Equally spectacular in other eyes are the world's largest aquatic plant, the Queen's Water Lily *Victoria regia;* red Fringed Hibiscus; red Cape Honeysuckle; African Violets; African Tulip Trees; Purple Honckenya; African Laburnum; Showy Combretum; Red Orchid Tree Bauhina. Other notables are those wondrous oddities such as Mimicry Plants, Lithops "Stones" imitating rocks around them; tree-like Aloes up to 60 feet high with masses of rosy-red racemes; Torch Lily *(Kniphofia uvaria),* Glory Lily *(Gloriosa superba),* African Lily *(Agapanthus africanus),* Kafir Lily *(Clivia miniata),* Candelabra Aloe, Peacock Iris *(Moraea pavonia),* Arizoaceae or Carpetweed Family, Tree Fuchsia, Castor Bean, Red Bottlebrush Greyis, and Kalanchoe members of Crassulaceae. East Africa astounds viewers with some of these same plants plus mountain peaks and valleys laden with Ferns to Raphia Palms; Orchids to Cycads; African Violets to woody Sausage Tree Kigelias.

Today the flower lover limited to a short trip to one area, would surely choose South Africa ... to the Zoological Gardens of Herman Eckstein Park or "The Wilds" reserve of native flora around the "Golden City," Johannesburg ... to Pretoria, "Flower of the Transvaal" during Jacaranda Week ... to that great wonder of the world, Victoria Falls on the Zambesi River with its wild masses of Blood Lily Haemanthus and lush vegetation ... to the Flower Market. Municipal Gardens of Cape Town and nearby National Botanical Gardens at Kirstenbosch ... to Durban for a Zulu Rickshaw ride amid subtropical flowers then by car to a magnificent 20,000-acre reserve which is a game and flower sanctuary — the Royal Natal National Park.

EAST PAKISTAN, INDIA, CHINA, INDONESIA, THAILAND, JAVA, SUMATRA, MALAYAN PENINSULA

Quaint camel caravans from overland bazaars of ancient Kabul, Kashmir, Lahore, Darjeeling, Rangoon, Calcutta, Canton or Saigon ... ships that sailed the Indian Ocean, Bay of Bengal and South China Seas to such marketplaces as Bombay, Macao, Hong Kong and Singapore — all helped early exchanges of plants, flowers and fruits between ancient cultures of the African and Asian continents with Western lands. Today's visitor, botanist or home gardener has difficulty in placing origins of some favorite flowers. Numerous species seem native to this vast Asia-Indonesian domain, Southern Iran, Afghanistan and Pakistan since caravan routes to India and China have blended flora.

INDIA is a colorful country from its rock-cut caves to Ajanta to its world-famous Taj Mahal ... from garden surrounded temples and mosques to ports and bazaars. It has more than twice the people but little more than half the size of the United States. Yet India manages to have room for botanic gardens and has been the origin of some of the most loved tropical flowers. Some flowers are credited only to India, such as Crossandra, Butterfly Pea Clitoria, Sky Vine Thumbergia, Woolly Morning Glory, Christmas Vine Porana and Jasmines such as Crape, Arabian and Primrose but most originate in an area that ranges into Burma, China and Malaysia.

MALAYAN monsoon regions of Burma, China, Malayan Peninsula and the East Indies create lush vegetation and rain forest growth. These areas are so similar, Orchids, Aroids and luxuriant plants spread from place to place growing like true natives being seen in abundance today — especially where cultivated. Thus Singapore — a crowded little island — is noted for Gladiolus and Orchids which actually originated in Burma, China and Malaya.

Rare and renowned plants such as the Giant Arum of Sumatra, the iridescent Peacock Plant of Burma or the weird Black Bat Flower and Golden Coconut from Malaya can be identified with one specific place of origin.

Pungent and fragrant Gingers are widespread. Nearly all originated in Tropical Asia and Africa but the most loved are from Asia, especially East Indies and South Pacific Islands. Other fragrant beauties from this area are the Llang Llang Canaga of East Indies, spicy Nutmeg Tree and Horseradish Tree, but Gingers are favored everywhere. Specific identity would be Red Ginger and Shell Ginger, Asiatic; Crape Ginger, Asiatic and Philippine; Torch Ginger from East Indies; White Ginger native to India and Malaya and Yellow Ginger from

India — botanists struggle while residents from all these places and South Sea Islands to Hawaii claim Gingers.

Orchids — some of the most unusual genera — come from these same localities. Moth Orchid Phalaenopsis originally ranged from Asia to East Indies; Vanda species from India to New Guinea; Paphiopedilum is the genus of Asiatic Lady Slippers that are tropical; Dendrobiums from the Malayan Peninsula; Cymbidiums from India to Australia; Phaius range from Asia and Africa to Pacific Islands and Australia; many of the Jewel Orchids grown for their foliage come from Borneo and Far East Islands; Spathoglottis grow from India to New Caledonia; Aerides are found from India to Malaysia and Japan; Arachnis and Grammatophyllum from Asia to Pacific Islands, as are Renanthera, Ascocentrums and Trichoglottis which are growing in favor with hobbyists and hybridizers.

BURMA and India are famous for Water Lilies, Lotus, Iris, Cyclamen, and Red Silk Cotton Bombax while Burma alone is the home of the rare Flame Amherstia with red flower sprays arching up to three feet. Its unusual but showy relative, Red Silk Albizia, with powder-puff flowers amid feathery leaves ranges from Iran to the Pacific Islands as does the yellow Woman's Tongue. Orchid Tree Bauhinias with red, purple or lavendar flowers are from India and China though the Hong Kong Bauhinia is most sought in the U.S. today, with the yellow and red Bauhinia shrub from Africa gaining.

Queen's Crape Myrtle is found from India to Australia as is the Jewel Vine but Golden Shower Cassias, Blue Sage, Orange Jasmine, and Crimson Ixoras range only from India to the East Indies. The Pomegranate is limited to Southern Asia while the Chenille Plant is found from Burma to the East Indies; Gardenias and Camellias from China and Japan (some are tropical, others temperate); some Roses and Rose Family members such as Chinese and Indian Hawthorn and Firethorn Pyracantha came from Southern China; Osbeckia from India and China; Java Rhododendron from Malaya; Crotons from the Fiji Islands to Australia while Thailand contributes Orchids, Pomaloes, Bananas and Hibiscus varieties and Jacob's Coat and Copperleaf Acalyphas come from the South Pacific Islands. The list can be endless stretching from tiny blossoms to giants . . . from Pagoda Flowers to Snapdragon Gmelinas to Australian oddities.

AUSTRALIA

AUSTRALIA — "sunshine continent" about same size as U.S.A. — offers an entirely new world for plant lovers. Australians spend most of their time outdoors and New South Wales is famous for its vegetation such as Waratah Telopea with its fire red four-inch flower heads.

Any place with fauna of kangaroo, koala bear, wallaby, platypus and kookaburra bird which allegedly laughs instead of singing . . . where farms are the size of some states and even some countries . . . where some neighbors are 124 miles apart so children learn by radio and doctors visit by plane . . . any place *this* unusual would be expected to have "fire plants" such as the "wild pear" which depends on forest fires for its seeds to propagate; and all sorts of different flora seen no place else originally, or recently, unless especially tended and imported.

Australian flora is estimated to consist of over 10,000 different species. Over 75 percent of these occur naturally nowhere else. There are some 600 species of Eucalyptus — blooms of flame red, yellow or white — but almost no coniferous trees. Australian forests have only the one genus — Eucalyptus. This surprises European and American visitors who feel this is the one monotonous sight here. Where it is too dry for these trees, Acacia shrubs grow. To be different these Acacias — 400 to 630 species — exchange delicate feathery leaves of seedling-youth to broad strange-formation of needle-like larger stalks when older. In flowering season Acacias are literally smothered in little scented yellow "mimosa-like" balls of flowers which make even the odd-growth-older-ones lovely. These delicate blossoms even lessen shock of its local name, "Golden Wattle."

Strange too are floral shapes of many Orchids and herbaceous plants such as "Kangaroo paws" with red and green and red flowers like toes of a paw, "fringed hare" orchids and antelope Dendrobium orchids. The Proteaceae family offers some of the most interesting flower-groups which are entirely different species from the South Africans. Dense magnificently colored tiny flowers form large and striking inflorescences with fruits developing to look like droll gnomes when they gape open.

Red Bottlebrushes are showy and vie with other arty-shapes and colors such as red or white Kahili flowers, Sea Urchin Hakea, Spikey Golden Honeysuckle and Scarlet Honeysuckle Banksias, Spectacular Firewheel Stenocarpus, Lavender Riceflower, Queen's Crape Myrtle, scarlet Glory Pea Clianthus, Jewel Vine Derris, Queensland Umbrella Purple Sarsaparilla, New South Wales Christmas Bush, Darling Pea Swainsonia, Manuka Tea, Bower-Plant Pandorea vine, weeping clusters of Tulipwood flowers that expend into showy fruits to pop open showing shiny jet-black seeds, red and yellow Moreton Bay Chestnut, Flame tree and Bangar nut tree which is planted along highways. Many of these flowers can be seen in Botanic Gardens at Sydney, Melbourne and Adelaide, whereas tropical Fern gullies (with Australian Tree Ferns to tiny relatives) and rain forests are a short distance from larger cities.

THE PHILIPPINES

THE PHILIPPINES — Land of 7,109 islands — is a treasure of floral riches, growing over 10,000 different flowering plants.

Petal to petal, almost endemic species share gardens with lovely introduced tropical flowers, for the total land area is slightly larger than Arizona or about as big as Italy. This flower region of 115,601 square miles — like petals floating on waves — spreads, island by island, over an area as large as Mexico.

Waling-Waling or the *Vanda sanderiana*, is the most famous of all Philippine orchids. Large soft brown and purplish tinted blossoms, of this highly valued and hybridized orchid, last a month on the plant and are esteemed by every orchid grower in the world.

"Paradise of Orchids" is a title often bestowed upon Hawaii, but botanically speaking, the Philippines deserve that crown. Only three small orchid species originated in Hawaii, while the Philippines have about 1,000 different orchid species growing wild. That famous Waling-Waling, Vanda ancestor with valuable hybrid offspring in prized collections around the world, lives as a wild flower *only* in a small area of Mindanao.

Cascades of white or pink Moth orchids, Phalaenopsis, are the ones most frequently seen, even hanging in large open windows of the poorest native palm leaves/bamboo hut, while fragrant species of purple Dendrobium orchids cling to trees, broadcasting heady scents into the air. Most Philippine flowers are more fragrant than those of other lands — or so it seems on these islands.

One rare ornamental family member rarely found elsewhere is 'Doña Aurora' *(Mussaenda philippica,* variety *Aurorae* of *Rubeaceae)* an ever-flowering white shrub with enlarged petals that only disappear when pruned off. There are hybrids of this in red and white with one red petal.

Red flowering trees are everywhere in the Philippines. They include the Tulip Tree *(Spathodea),* deep red Dapdap *(Erythrina),* silk cotton tree and Fire trees *(Delonix).*

. One of the loveliest greenhouse flowers is a small (to 3 ft.) Philippine shrub *Medinilla magnifica* which has hanging pink or coral flowers on terminal sprays enhanced by showy pink bracts and glossy evergreen leaves.

The Jade Vine, *Strongylodon macrobotrys,* has drooping curved flower clusters up to three feet in length the color of its namesake gemstone only more lustrous which blooms all spring and summer. This flower is one of the newer rare imports showing floral treasures still to be hunted and introduced into other lands.

PLANT HUNTERS

Unexplored areas excite humankind. Questions — unanswered — breed discontent ... fire wanderlust. Adventurers must see "what's on the other side" — whether it is beyond our atmosphere ... on the "dark" side of the moon or a continent ... in pure science test tubes or hybridization ... or as yet uncharted areas of this earth. These people become pioneers — fortunately some are plant lovers too.

Plants traveled long before man consciously sought them. Their seeds flew with birds, floated on winds, sailed oceans or hitch-hiked on animals and early hunters. Mysterious ways and qualities of plants intrigued men as soon as they had time to think.

Mysteries — for as long as they exist — will draw men into danger to discover what is new or different. So it was — and is — with plant hunters.

One of our first documented plant hunting expeditions occurred in Egypt about 5,000 years ago, when Pharaoh Sankhkarra sent ships to the Gulf of Aden for Cinnamon and Cassia. On the walls of the great Karnak Temple vivid paintings depict multi-oared sailing ships Queen Hatshepsut's slaves are loading with balled-and-basketed Incense Trees. Other trees line the decks. By planned hunting and conquest, Egyptians collected, then cultivated most of the useful and beautiful plants of the Middle East. Finally — in much the same way — Greek and Roman warriors took over these exotic flowers and fruits. Eventually these tropical botanical treasures spread all over Europe, and England, eventually to the West Indies, Americas and the whole world.

European monks grew herbs, grapes and flowers which they carried to monasteries in England and other countries. Thus when Crusaders went to Africa, they carried herbs for their physicians and found more rarities growing where, in time, Portuguese, Spanish, Greek and Dutch sailors traded with overland caravans from the Far East. Commerce began between Royal Houses. Henry VIII really started the world race to obtain rare plants but other countries were busy botanically.

The Spanish Crown contributed Plant Hunters too. From Columbus' 1492 voyage ... to writers like Gonzalo Fernandez de Oviedo (1526) to expedition by order of Philip II for his physician Francisco Hernandez to study New World Flora in 1570. This was the first purely botanical expedition and just one of many by the Spanish including those by Jose Celestino Mutis, famous botanist-astronomer gathering much in 33 years work, and Martin Sesse — to a scientific revival in Spain reigned over by Philip V. Spanish Jesuits taught at San Marcos and a Spaniard introduced the Linnean system to the Viceroyalty of New Grenada. Botany became an established science at Hispo-American Universities. Sweden's great Linnaeus not only contributed a naming system but also discovered better methods of safely transporting seeds and plants used by all countries. German and Dutch botanists contributed ideas and traded with French, Portuguese and English.

Queen Elizabeth's reign created greater trade with the world. Famous London Gardener-Writer John Gerard (1545-1612) sent out plant collectors and exchanged plants with various diplomats. Fruits and medicinal plants got priorities but rare flowers were collected too with new ones bringing the highest prices — even as today. By 1577 Dean of Windsor William Harrison could write in his *Description of England,* "Strange herbs, plants and annual fruits are daily brought unto us from the Indies, America, 'Ceylon', Canary Isles and all parts of the world."

Sir Joseph Banks created the greatest scientific expedition in 1768 with Captain Cook on the *HMS Endeavour.* He and his hand-picked assistants started a "Golden Age in Horticulture" even though they could not bring living plants from the South Seas. These Plant Hunters escaped storms, hostile natives and near starvation — in some months someone died nearly every day — to bring botanical discoveries and news back to England. Sir Joseph Banks continued his devotion as a leader for over 50 years. As Director of Kew Royal Gardens, he saw that others such as the first King's Botanist Francis Masson, searched for new plants for British stovehouses. The Bird-of-Paradise was probably the most exciting of Masson's South African early discoveries for the Royal Gardens at Kew.

In these early days, Plant Hunters' notes could not even begin to tell innumerable dangers they braved. Storms at sea were surpassed by maggots and weevils in their skimpy food. Frustrations of mildew and rot in plants for which they risked limb and life ashore among wild animals — often wilder savages who set lion or buffalo traps with deadly spikes to impale beast or man. On the same around-the-world-trip (1776-1780) when natives killed Captain Cook, Botanist David Nelson had no fresh beef, nor flour nor news from home for three years. Death was near constantly. Then they anchored in Macao and Nelson was able to visit Canton where Chinese nurserymen had grown flowering plants for hundreds of years. Plants he shipped from here as well as his other discoveries induced Sir Joseph to select Nelson seven years later for a trip aboard the *Bounty* with Lieutenant Bligh for an ill-fated cruise.

For the first time in history, a Royal Navy Ship was designed or converted into a floating garden-conservatory to carry Breadfruit trees from Tahiti to Jamaica in the West Indies to furnish food for slaves. The Captain's Greatcabin and stern decks were made into a plant-storage-house-"official"-Garden — even so marked for all to see. History knows how Bligh fared but Plant Hunter Nelson died of fever and exposure from that 3,518 mile sea struggle in a tiny cockleboat. Sir Joseph did not send another collector overseas from Kew for 10 years after Nelson's death but did receive plants and seeds from travellers and Embassies in the Far East and Africa. In 1803 another Scotsman, William Kerr, was sent to China where Sir Joseph had found Magnolias, Hydranges and Roses; and dedicated men such as George Caley and Dr. John Livingstone sent specimens home. Kerr was to send many new Azaleas, Gardenias, Camellias and such botanical prizes while exchanging rare fruits with the Chinese.

Sir Joseph continued to send collectors to all parts of the world but a growing number of dedicated men in the new Horticultural Society of London were also sending out collectors. Although they lost the first two out of three of their Plant Hunters and heard constant news of other deaths, eager Plant Hunters appeared and eager Patrons continued to sponsor expeditions. Healthy young 22 and 23 year old gardeners died often; plants died by the thousands on these long voyages. Researchers wrote books on better methods of transporting plants, but, without any modern inventions, plants suffered. Men did too for they hacked their way through fever and snake ridden jungles without any modern drugs, specifically packaged foods nor water purifiers. Yet men such as James Bowie, Allen Cunningham, John Potts and John Forbes continued to travel far corners — and die hunting plants.

Horticultural Society of London Botanist-leaders were convinced importations of seeds and plant specimens were worth all risks. John Lindley records that during George III's reign, over 6,746 rare exotics were introduced successfully. The Society selected another Scot, young 23-year-old George Don to collect from three unsearched continents and islands in between. He searched and created great excitement in horticultural circles. In 1824 Don wrote of "rare and beautiful plants ... all of them deserving of being cultivated in our stoves ... many may be seen growing in Gardens of the Horticultural Society at Cheswick". These included *Clematis grandiflora, Gardenia coccinea, Cassia conspicua,* Orchids and five Clerodendrons. "Several of them," Don continued, "I've been so fortunate as to introduce into the country in a living state" — this master understatement indicated an almost epoch-making event in exotic plant introductions. Don accomplished all these discoveries in what was then an extremely short expedition of 15 months — most took more than twice that time on great sailing ships and brought back dead plants.

Next great Plant Hunter was David Douglas. In 1823, young Douglas was scheduled to go to China but political upheavals there caused him to be sent to the United States. Douglas is credited with introducing more trees and plants to British gardens than most other Plant Hunters but most were from North America's Pacific Coast, redwood forests, down into California — therefore rarely tropical. A distinguished 11 years later — after escaping an Indian plague in Fort Vancouver, nearly losing his life in a canoeing disaster where he did lose his equipment and 400 plant specimens — Douglas sailed to Hawaii where his curiosity led to his death. He and his little terrier set out one day to explore the side of Mauna Loa volcano. He fell into a pit into which a young bullock had already fallen. It's speculated that Douglas looked into the pit and the edge gave way. In any event he was found in the pit evidently trampled to death by the raging injured bullock.

While Douglas roamed the western Hemisphere, English and European horti-culturists admired temperate plants he discovered but dreamed of having more rare exotics so very difficult to grow in their stove-houses but even harder to transport successfully from tropical lands.

Secrets destined to revolutionize plant transportation were discovered by a Dr. Nathaniel B. Ward. As an amateur naturalist he placed a butterfly chrysalis in a large bottle of leaf mould and put a lid over it. In a couple of weeks, he noticed some seedling Fern and Grass sprouting in this bottle. Dr. Ward forgot the butterfly when he realized the excitement of his discovery. The soil stayed moist because moisture was drawn up by the heat of day then condensed on sides of the bottle to slide back down, forming a continuous degree of humidity. His Fern and Grass prospered for four years so Dr. Ward decided to experiment further with this phenomenon. He knew of the disasters plantsmen had trying to transport living specimens from foreign shores therefore he designed two cases. They were shaped like former plant-cabins but based on the principle of his original bottle with all glass sides and top, strengthened and sealed at corners and edges — a miniature greenhouse. He filled these cases with ferns and grasses then shipped them to Australia. They arrived in perfect condition so these plants were removed and the cases filled with *Gleichenia microphylla* and *Callicoma serratifolia*. They travelled on the ships' decks with a temperature range of up to 100 degrees in Sydney to 20 degrees at Cape Horn while decks were covered with snow soaring to 100 degrees at Rio and 120 crossing the Equator arriving eight months later in 40 degree chill of the English Channel. The plants arrived in their Wardian case hothouses in vigorous health although they were never watered after leaving Sydney.

A whole new Golden Era (or should that be Platinum Era?) opened when

(Continued on page 71)

Descriptions of the following pictures

Page 49

African Tulip Tree *(Spathodea campanulata)*

Flame of the Forest is another common name for this evergreen tree which blooms during the winter months. Masses of scarlet bell-shaped blossoms open toward the sun. In its native home of Tropical Africa it grows to a height of 50 to 60 feet. A near relative (S. nilotica) *also produces crimson-scarlet blooms larger than a tea cup and in bunches. The tree resembles the African Tulip Tree except in having hairy rough leaves instead of deep green glossy-smooth leaves.*

Page 50

Frangipani, Temple Tree *(Plumeria rubra* and *Plumeria alba)*

Fragrance plus beauty caused this small tree to be a favorite in planting near temples and burying grounds ... hence, its common name of Temple Tree. Centuries before white men found this tree, Aztec Indians used the flowers as religious rite offerings and anyone touching them or smelling them after the rites was put to death. The showy, funnel-shaped, fragrant blossoms of white, red or yellow were named after French Botanist Charles Plumier who made many voyages to Central and South America in the 17th century. These trees are native to the West Indies and Tropical America but are found in both East and West Indies, Ceylon and Hawaii where blossoms are used for leis to adorn visitors' necks. Its fragrant waxy blossoms are seen on Caribbean Islands and may also have originated in East Indies but usually are credited to the tropical Americas. Many specific and varietal names have been given to the numerous color forms but are now regarded as one species — P. rubra. *However, some garden lovers are continuing to call the white,* P. alba *or* P. acuminata *and the red,* P. rubra.

Page 50 (lower left)

Golden Frangipani, Temple Tree *(Plumeria rubra)*

Fragrance plus beauty makes any Frangipani popular and accounted for its being a favorite for planting near temples and burying grounds by various Indians such as the Aztecs. This golden variation is especially prized but colors of Frangipanis range from white to a deep red. Many specific and varietal names have been given to various color forms.

(Continued on page 65)

AFRICAN TULIP TREE

PLUMERIA RUBRA ↑
←

FRANGIPANI,
TEMPLE TREE

PLUMERIA ALBA

For detailed description see page 48

FLOSS-SILK TREE, CHORISIA

GOLDEN SHOWER, CASSIA

ROYAL POINCIANA, FLAMBOYANT

53

For detailed description see page 66

SAGO PALM, MALE CYCAD INFLORESCENCE

CHACONIA

DWARF POINCIANA

CHINESE HIBISCUS

WHITE HIBISCUS

56

CRAPE MYRTLE, QUEEN FLOWER

PINK POUI TREE

For detailed description see page 67

GOLD TREE,
YELLOW POUI

ORCHID TREE
BAUHINIA

RED BOTTLE
BRUSH TREE

CANDLEBUSH

CHENILLE PLANT

For detailed description see page 69

RED SILK COTTON TREE,
BOMBAX

61

MORNING GLORY

POTATO BUSH, MORNING GLORY BUSH

POINSETTIA

For detailed description see page 70

(Continued from page 48)

Descriptions of the foregoing pictures

Page 51

Floss-Silk Tree, Chorisia *(Chorisia speciosa)*

Pink Floss-Silk blossoms appear like a pink cloud in a blue sky when this lovely tree bursts into bloom in late fall and winter. Growing to 50 feet tall, Chorisias create an enormous show with large 3-4" five petal flowers covering each leafless branch. Leaves unfold after flowering, but this will not be for several weeks to a month since that's how long flowering lasts. Chorisias were named for Botanical Artist Ludwig Choris. Extremely thorny trucks probably kept this artist at bay just as they do anyone trying to collect a flower blossom today. Originally from Brazil they grow today in most tropical regions of the world and in the U.S. from Florida to Texas and California.

Page 52

Golden Shower, Shower of Gold, Cassia *(Cassia fistula)*

Golden Shower shrubs or trees have large clusters of bright yellow blossoms which seem to cascade down the limbs in grape-like bunches. The flowers have five petals with long curving stamens and pistil that stick out from the center of the bloom. Also known as the Indian laburnum, this lovely tree originated in India but is extensively grown in all warm parts of the world today.

Page 53

Flamboyant, Royal Poinciana *(Delonix regia)*

Igniting the skies with flames of red, this strikingly beautiful tree is considered a native of Madagascar but is equally at home in the Caribbean. In fact, it was named for M. de Poinci, a governor of the French West Indies, and was growing wild in Jamaica in 1756. Its scarlet long-clawed petal blossoms measure three to four inches across and are touched with yellow and white. They cover the wide-spreading limbs of trees which reach a height of sixty feet. The spectacular show of blooms also individually resemble orchids. These are followed by dangling pods often two feet long which are sometimes used as fuel in native fires ... and fuel for verbal battles when men, hearing the breeze-borne clatter of these pods, call the tree "women's tongues."

← BANANA BLOSSOM

Page 54

Male Cycad Inflorescence *(Cycas revoluta* "Sago Palm"*)*

Male cones of the Sago Palm show small flowers between scales centered in the rosette of leaves. Geologically very ancient, these are "living fossils" of the plant world. This is probably the commonest Cycad used in landscape plantings. It is almost universally called Sago Palm in spite of the fact that it does not produce commercial sago for puddings and starch in textiles nor is it a palm. It is only palm-like with its glossy-green leaves arching at the tips. It is native to South Japan.

Page 55 (top)

Chaconia, Wild Poinsettia *(Warszewiczia coccinea)*

Vermilion clusters spray out on long arching branches, its bright scarlet racemes — up to 4 feet long — create a startling splash of color against its darker green foliage. It is found abundantly in Trinidad's forests and is Trinidad's National Flower. Its name, Chaconia, commemorates the last Spanish Governor of Trinidad, General Chacon. "Water Well Tree" is another name because it must have plenty of water and blooms in the summer wet season. It is most commonly called Wild Poinsettia (away from Trinidad), but this plant is not related to the Christmas Poinsettia although there are many similarities in its flaming beauty.

Page 55 (lower)

Dwarf Poinciana *(Poinciana pulcherrima)*

Often called Flame Poinciana, Barbados Pride and Bush Poinciana, it grows all over the Tropical Americas and its exact origin is still being debated. The feathery compound leaves are deciduous on the 12 to 15 ft. rather thorny shrub but the flashing red or yellow flowers appear practically all year long.

Page 56 (top)

Chinese Hibiscus, Garden Red Hibiscus *(Hibiscus rosa-sinensis)*

"Leading lady" all over the Tropical Worlds is the Hibiscus whose native country is not definitely known but is credited to China or Japan. Red is probably the commonest color but yellow is almost equally popular. Recently, a white and green variegated leaf variety has become popular from the original stock plant in Trinidad's Royal Botanic Gardens, it flourishes all through the islands to Jamaica. Most flowers are a showy 4½ to 5 inches in diameter. There are double varieties too.

Page 56 (lower)

White Hibiscus *(Hibiscus rosa-sinensis* 'Ruth Wilcox'*)*

Hibiscus are so colorful and free flowering that few tropical gardens are without several. Most of the present-day varieties and hybrids trace their origins to the great bushes of Chinese Hibiscus (Hibiscus rosa-sinensis) *or Rose-of-China growing 15 to 20 feet high. Blooms on most last only a day — except on this Ruth Wilcox (and a few yellows) which holds for two days.*

Page 57

Crape Myrtle, Queen of Flowers, Queen Flower, Crape or Flower Crape *(Lagerstroemia indica,* also *L. speciosa,* and *L. flos-reginae)*

Tight pink clusters 4 to 9 inches long adorn bushes and trees in this genus in showy masses. Scientists argue the name with L. speciosa *preferred. Size of the plant decides the botanical name (up to 20 feet tall the Crape Myrtle is known as* L. indica *from China; a tree up to 50 or 60 feet tall is called* L. speciosa *or* L. flos-reginae *from India-Australia areas called Queen's Crape Myrtle) but popularly all of these are loved and called Queen Flowers.*

Page 58

Pink Poui Tree, Pink Trumpet, Pink Tecoma, Apamata, Tabebuia *(Tabebuia pentaphylla* or *Tecoma pentaphylla)*

Giant bouquet of pinkish-rose petunia-like trumpets cover this West Indies native. It blooms when only 3 feet tall on up to when it is a 60 foot tree. Lavishly ornamental, it is useful too. Perhaps its use as an excellent shade tree for cocao and coffee bushes helped it become widespread and popular early in history but its beauty makes it a favorite for garden, street and park planting now. When the blossoms fall they lay a carpet of color on the ground. As a tree, it is used for excellent commercial wood.

Page 59 (top)

Yellow Poui, Gold Tree *(Tecoma serratifolia, Tabebuia argentea)*

Gold does grow on trees! When these golden trumpet-shaped blossoms open in masses of shining glory, it's as if a Master-Jeweler polished each to sparkle in tropic sunlight and make the entire tree an enormous golden yellow free-form sphere. Silver leaves composed of 5 to 7 leaflets make this a lovely tree even when not in bloom. In some areas the tree is usually leafless when in bloom; in others new leaves quickly replace fallen leaves. They are now grown in most tropical and subtropical countries where temperatures rarely reach freezing. Spring or late winter also brings blossoms on its near relative T. pentaphylla while T. pallida opens in midspring. All of these are being used as street plantings in more and more cities.

Page 59 (lower)

Orchid Tree, Bauhinia, Poor Man's Orchid *(Bauhinia variegata)*

Corsage orchids seem to grow on trees when these come into profuse bloom. In fact, when these blossoms are created into a corsage they truly become a "poor man's orchid." Twin lobed leaves gave this its name to commemorate the brothers Bauhin, 16th century herbalists. Native to India, this tree has "gone native" all over the Tropical World.

Page 60 (top)

Red Bottle Brush Tree *(Callistemon lanceolatus)*

Weeping willow type branches of this tree are adorned with bristly cylindrical spikes 2-4" long of red flowers that look exactly like brushes used to clean baby bottles — except that they are scarlet. Odd inflorescences are composed of separated spikes of red flowers with numerous dominant red stamens sticking out all around the stem. Usually a small tree, it may grow to 25 feet with long, narrow greyish green leaves. Originally from Australia, the Red Bottle Brush Tree thrives in the Caribbean, Bahamas, most of Florida, Bermuda as well as Asia and South Pacific Islands. C. speciosus has very dense spikes with showy red stamens tipped with a yellow anther and is the handsomest of all. Callistemon is Greek for beautiful stamens. This curiosity — Bottle Brush blooms — makes a lovely tree with branches arching over like a fountain.

Page 60 (lower)

Candlebush, Golden Candle, Acapulco, Candlestick Senna *(Cassia alata)*

Named, of course, because its inflorescences begin as erect spikes of candle-like clusters of bright yellow buds on curved candelabra-like stems. Flowers open from the base upward over a period of several weeks. It can attain a height of 15 feet and is truly striking when tight buds keep the cylindrical shape or open into fluffy "suns." Native to Tropical America.

68

Page 61 (top)

Chenille Plant, Red Hot Cat-Tails, Monkey Tails *(Acalypha hispida)*

Streamers of dark reddish-purple fur-like or chenille-like blooms give its common names. These "cat-tails" often hang down in large groups as much as 18 inches from the green textured heart-shaped leaves. Flowers without petals actually make up the tassels which certainly look "fake" until seen and felt. Bushes are usually small but can grow to 10 ft. The catkin flowers are long lasting. Grows in sun or shade but richer color when grown in the sun. Reported to be from East Indies or Burma.

Page 61 (lower)

Red Silk Cotton Tree Bloom *(Bombax ceiba)*

Large shiny red blooms appear when the Bombax tree is leafless, creating quite a show. After flowering, finger-fashioned leaflets unfold in coppery-green hues. Later the capsule fruit shows seeds embedded in a fluffy mass of silk or cotton-like hairs which are used commercially in some parts of the world as kapok to stuff cushions. Bombax is Latin for cotton or cotton wadding, hence its name. It has relatives nearby in other colors but the Red Silk Cotton Tree has more men admirers while the Pink seems to have greater appeal for ladies. It has had many botanical names in the past but was recently re-identified.

Page 62 (top)

Morning Glory *(Ipomoea Learii)*

Perky perennial, this widely-grown tropical vine produces masses of purple flowers. It is a quick growing twiner and will trail along the ground rooting at nodes. If broken off but left on the ground, it will bloom from this new plant in several months.

Page 62 (lower)

Potato Bush, Morning Glory-Bush *(Ipomoea carnea)*

Large showy trumpet-shaped flowers are rather flimsy in the wind but delicate mauvish-pink petals flow into deeper colors within the throat and can be enjoyed all day. This perennial, with its bushy habit, is a Tropical American native found abundantly over the countryside and in village gardens. It is so common and so commonly called Potato Bush that few people know its botanical name. Ipomoea crassicaulis *is also called the Bush Morning Glory and is cultivated from Peru to Mexico and Texas.*

Page 63

Poinsettia, Fire Plant, Painted Leaf *(Poinsettia pulcherrima* or *Euphorbia pulcherrima)*

Yuletide symbol, these flaming beauties bloom over a six months' period in protected areas. Actually a shaggy head of leaves forms the red aureole or halo about its inconspicuous yellow flowers with the Ubangi lips in the center. This flower is termed a native of Mexico but has "gone native" in most of the Old World Tropics. The double red variety, P. plenissima, *has larger blooms and lasts longer on the plant.*

Page 64

Banana Blossom *(Musa sapientum* and *M. Cavendishii sp.)*

This is an unusual tropical flower that turns into fruit. A dark red torch-like pointed inflorescence shoots out on a long stem from the lush stalk then arches over. The fleshy red bracts fold and curl back revealing rows of creamish-yellow flowers which gradually turn into curved upside down green then swell into yellow bananas. There are many varieties of these species but 'Canary,' 'Gros Michel' and 'Lady Fingers' are favored depending upon space available and grower's tastes. All require regular watering or low moist spots in the garden. These "blossoms" also make striking flower arrangements. There are many other bananas, but these and M. paradisiaca *are well known and probably all originally natives of Tropical Asia.* M. maurelii *comes from Ethiopia;* M. ensete *from moist Central and East Africa; others from Burma-Ceylon area.*

(Continued from page 47)

these Wardian cases brought Gleichenia alive into England. Plant Hunters' dreams and visions of floral treasures of the exotic tropics could now be brought in — not as dull dried herbarium specimens — but as living plants ready to burst into magic bloom! The sixth Duke of Devonshire and his Gardener Joseph Paxton immediately dreamed of having a fabulous tree of India, *Amherstia nobilis,* in the Great Conservatory at Chatsworth House. To secure this tree no one in England had in their garden, in fact, few had even seen, they chose 24-year-old under-gardener-bachelor John Gibson. Gibson learned quickly and sent many treasures home from danger filled expeditions. He was to "spare no expense" to secure the finest plants. Orchids and houseplants the British world had never seen arrived by the Wardian caseful from Gibson but it took near heartbreak and over two years to secure one live *Amherstia nobilis* sprig. He proudly "baby-sat" it all the way home, nursing it above his own health, to arrive green. This would not have survived without Dr. Ward's miniature greenhouse ... the "orchid craze" could not have started in England.

"They (the Wardian cases) have been the means," said Sir William Hooker, writing from Kew in 1856, "in the last 15 years of introducing more new and valuable plants to our gardens than were imported during the preceding century." Certainly an even greater era for Plant Hunters loomed ahead ... but Plant Hunters who dared brave the past can not be forgotten — not so long as *one* tropical blossom can be seen in bloom away from its native land.

FAMILIES OF TROPICAL FLOWERS AND PLANTS

Plants, like people, are all different, all interesting...and — all need understanding and love to cultivate.

Our Green World of plants is divided into five primary plant groups: algae; fungi; mosses/liverworts; ferns/fern allies; and flowering plants. The first four groups are vital to our eco-system but are non-flowering. We could not do without any of them but rarely are they privately cultivated. Generally speaking, only the last two — ferns/fern allies and flowering plants — are the ones worth knowing for beauty's sake, peace of mind, hobbies for rest and relaxation.

Knowing even a little about them takes effort but increases interest. Today over 350,000 different kinds of plant organisms, of Species, are recognized in the plant world. Each Species is gathered into a closely related collection to make a Genus; each Genus is gathered into a collection of closely related Genera to form a Family.

A Botanical Family, thus, may mean thousands upon thousands of individual flowers...such as the Orchid Family with over 25,000 species and more hybrids or the Pea Family with 12,000 members.

Houseplants are brought into homes for benefits to humankind, just as gardens outdoors are created. Indoors and outdoors, these flowers become part of our families — but each individual species also has a family of its own.

Houseplants available from today's nurseries represent approximately 118 Botanical Families. Some ferns are included in that count but some flowers and flowering trees are excluded, due to extremely difficult culture problems, lack of hardiness or size. Few houseplants tolerate cold zones. Most are warmth-loving, being happy and comfortable where their human friends are comfortable.

Giant tropical relatives to houseplants, such as flowering trees, are seen to best advantage in their native habitats or in countries where they have been introduced in large numbers. At times a native is ignored or, at least, not fully appreciated on its own home grounds but will be venerated and make a lavish showing when purposely introduced to another place. For instance, Royal Poinciana *(Delonix regia)* trees have been 75 percent burned out of their original homeland, Madagascar...yet magnificent avenues of these flamboyant trees are grown in the Philippines, Hawaii and Florida. Five families — Orchids, Bromeliads, Ginger, Cacti/Succulents and Anthuriums/Aroids — will be discussed separately later as "Favorite Families."

THE BANANA FAMILY *(Musaceae)* has only about 125 species and 5 or 6 genera but such striking and brilliant inflorescences or such delicious fruit that this family is highly prized for its economical and ornamental value. Flowers peek or pop out of boat-shaped, bird-in-flight or odd shaped bracts such as in the amazing Bird-of-Paradise Strelitzias or Lobster Claw Heliconias. A few of the plants have woody stems but almost all are soft tree-like stalks with huge paddle-shaped leaves.

THE BIGNONIA FAMILY *(Bignoniaceae)* has spectacular vines, shrubs and trees of over 600 species and 100 genera. Massive clusters of flowers are bell-shaped or tubular in a wide range of colors from the flaming red African Tulip Spathodea to blue-lavender Jacaranda to Golden Trumpet trees and from Flame Vine Pyrostegia fires to delicate pinks in Bower-Plant Pandorea to dark rose of the Sarita. Curious fruits make some more famous than their pretty

72

flowers, such as: the Sausage Tree with its strange woody fruits that look exactly like large sausages hanging from the limbs; or the Calabash Tree hard-shell fruits used to make maracas; and the Candle Trees.

THE GLOXINIA FAMILY *(Gesneriaceae)* is a large family with small jewel plants. In the 1700's Linnaeus could only describe four genera. Today over 500 species and over 80 genera plus numerous hybrids and mutations abound in nurseries and homes. The species are so varied in growth and flowering habits plus variables in foliage of velvetry to shiny textures only a taxonomist can place them on sight in the same family. Some have tuberous roots; others have fibrous roots or scaly rhizomes. Most can be propagated by leaf or stem cuttings; divisions; and seeds. After propagation, they can easily bloom within the year. Flowers are wheel-shaped, tubular or bell-shaped in colors of African Violet blues and pinks to Gloxinia (or Sinningia) lavenders and wine-reds to Columnea and Episcia bright reds against silvery-veined velvet leaves.

THE PEA FAMILY *(Leguminosae)* is a colorful giant family with members famous as ornamental trees, shrubs, vines, annual and perennial herbs. Quite a few genera are economically famous too for food, dye, oil, gum and timber. It is the third largest family with some 12,000 species and 600 genera. Graceful feathery leaves adorn some trees and shrubs that also have bright red or yellow powder-puff blossoms or dancing poinciana shapes. Others, Bauhinias, look like orchids and are, in fact, called "poor man's orchid" because of their shape, color and fact that they are often growing wild near cities. Some flowers masquerade as something else such as the Candlebush Cassias while many stay sweet-pea shaped and others become showers of gold or pink. The Pea Family is so varied . . . one of the most flamboyant members is the rare Flame Amherstia with flower sprays arching 3 feet into the air.

THE AMARYLLIS FAMILY *(Amaryllidaceae)* has 1200 species and 90 genera, mainly from South America, South Africa and Mediterranean but Holland now exports huge quantities of the bulbous lily-like types. Members of this family are perennial herbs, some having fibrous roots or rhizones but mostly, large bulbs when grown. These prized ornamentals have stalks of flowers with 3 inner petals and 3 outer sepals which may all be the same size or vary greatly. Most look so much like lilies their common names include it — Milk-and-Wine Lily with 12 to 30 blooms, Kafir Lily, Rain Lily, Barbados Lily, Jacobean Lily, Hurricane Lily and Amazon Lily, even when they are varied genera. The Blood Lily Haemanthus is different in that its 80 to 100 flowers are smaller and clustered in a round powder-puff ball. It is hard to believe, but the Century Plant Agave is also a family member.

THE SILKY OAK FAMILY *(Proteaceae)* contains shrubs and small trees primarily from Australia and South Africa. Flowers are beautifully odd mostly in racemes or heads up to 12 inches wide, on King Protea, for instance, with sweet syrupy nectar. Some have downy or spiky clusters of flowers looking like pin-wheel fireworks in bright reds and golden yellows or spectacular combinations of color in peculiar designs.

THE MADDER FAMILY *(Rubiaceae)* supplies many widely planted ornamentals plus coffee and quinine plants among its over 5,000 species and 450 genera of tropical herbs, shrubs, vines and trees. Flowers may be small and borne in cluster heads such as popular Crimson Ixoras, or singly such as Gardenias. Many are highly fragrant and most are easy growers. One of the showiest is Chaconia, native to Trinidad and Central America into Peru. Chaconia splashes vermillion racemes up to four feet long.

IRIS FAMILY *(Iridaceae)* members all show a striking family resemblance although some are larger or more glamorous. Tiger Flowers *(Tigridia pavonia)* have been widely cultivated and admired since the Aztecs ate these nutlike bulbs after enjoying their flower-view. Records also show Europeans grew Tiger Flowers in the 16th Century. The flower is abundant in the wilds throughout Guatemala and Mexico as well as cultivated actively. At the start of their rainy season, leaves push up and the flower stalk emerges. Each morning, red, violet, yellow or white flowers with contrasting spots open then fade in the early evening but each morning for 2 to 3 months new 3 to 6 inch flowers appear. The yellow Walking Iris is another favorite of this family but smaller.

THE DOGBANE FAMILY *(Apocynaceae)* despite its name, is one of man's best friends in producing beneficial drugs, some of which also help dogs, including: Periwinkles recently discovered source of drug for blood cancer; Rauwolfia for excellent tranquilizers and other alkaloids. Among this family's 1,500 species and 250-300 genera giving raw materials for use such as, Dyera yields basic for bubble gum, asbestos and linoleum; Funtumia provides rubber; Carissa has edible fruits, raw and in preserves but is also a showy fragrant shrub that even does well in windy salt sprayed seaside plantings. Many of the showiest flowers have toxic or poisonous parts, for instance, the popular and almost ever-blooming Oleanders in dark pinks, yellows, reds and whites and fragrant Wintersweet Acokanthera. Most spectacular is the Herald's Trumpet, Beaumontia grandiflora, vine with its enormous flower clusters. Yellow Allamanda vines run a close second in splash while forms of Purple Allamanda are becoming more popular since they can be flowered in pots and smaller spaces. Crape Jasmine stays a popular ornamental glossy-leaved plant with contrasting white blossoms which become so fragrant at night. Another sweet scented genus, Plumeria or Frangipani has long been sacred as a Temple offering by Aztecs in its native lands from Mexico to South America and it is now widespread in Hawaii, India and Florida.

ACANTHUS FAMILY *(Acanthaceae)* has some of the loveliest tropical vines in that rare color — blue. The Sky Vine, Thumbergia grandiflora blooms nearly all year with broadly flared bell-shaped flowers and rough textured leaves. Other Thumbergia flowers are white, yellow with a dark center, darker or paler blues. There are 2,000 species and 200 genera of herbs, small shrubs and vines. Some have flowers in bright spikes or cupped by spiny bracts that may be showier than flowers in reds, oranges, lavendars, violets and pinks. Quite a few members of this family are prized ornamentals and houseplants with Beloperone the most characteristic.

THE TOMATO FAMILY *(Solanaceae)* has a strange assortment in its over 2,000 species and 75 genera splashed over tropics into temperate zones including showy tropical flowers such as Scarlet Datura, Angel's Trumpet, Devil's Trumpet, Chalice Vine, Cup Flowers, Chameleon-like blue Brunfelsia, Marmalade Bush ... to infamous poisons and drugs such as Belladonna and Jimsonweed. Also in this family are internationally recognized tomato, potato, eggplant and tobacco plants.

There are over 85 prominent tropical plant families to be admired in gardens and travels to foreign lands. Naturally some special ones become favorites.

FAVORITE TROPICAL FLOWERS

ORCHIDS — Aristocrats of the Plant World; Royalty of the Flower World — fascinate and excite admirers more than most flora.

Symbols of glamour, mystery and opulence for centuries, orchids reign today as one of the world's favorites — gaining in popularity like the prettiest, sweetest baby in a kindergarten.

Orchids *deserve* legions of admirers for a myriad of reasons. They have the largest, most diverse and interesting family (overtaking the Compositae or Daisy Family a few years ago.) To date over 25,000 species are listed and described with equally that many, if not more, hybrids named and registered — plus new horizons yet to be discovered in hybridization and new wild species hiding in unexplored regions. Scientists cannot predict how many new crosses can be made between species, genera and hybrids — possibilities still existing are virtually unlimited, unimaginable today.

A Floral-Kaleidoscope — the Orchid Family — surely offers something fascinating for anyone/everyone! Except for modern Mericlones (which are actually pieces of original plants) no two orchids are exactly alike even when from the same seed-pot yet all have the same flower structure (least of their charms.) All orchid flowers have three sepals and three petals with one petal being so different in shape and/or color that it is usually called a "lip" or depending on form, "pouch," or "bucket." There are orchid plants only a fraction of an inch with flowers pinhead-size to fingernail-size; some have one or two blooms up to 9″ across; some are borne in massive colorful sprays; some will grow two stories high like "trees" than shoot out a thousand-bud flower stalk 10 to 15 feet long. Colors? There are no colors nor color combinations ever dreamed up by an artist (except black) to surpass the variety found in orchids.

No artist…no architect…no experimenter on a "drug trip"…no Walt Disney animator could create any figures, shapes and sizes more abstract, more vivid, more unique than orchids already have produced. Queens of this Royal Family are Cattleyas and Cattleya hybrids — the popular "corsage" orchids. However, various others are also popular while still more are gaining in popularity — at least seven different genera and hybrids vie for prestige today. Like a "back-sliding dieter in a candy store," hobbyists must strain to choose which orchids they want to grow — restraining their desires seeming even harder. There are orchids that grow in water; orchids that grow and even bloom underground; orchids with nothing but a star-like cluster of silver-gray roots until their fragrant silver-dollar-size blossoms with Mandarin-mustache-like curls pop out in ghost-white loveliness against jungle greens; orchids that mimic...looking like dancing dolls, small kites, monkeys, spiders, bees, butterflies, scorpions, birds in flight, pigeons on a fence, gingerbread men, "Punch and Judy" puppets, doves in a grotto, even a baseball glove or a catcher's mitt, a scared rabbit and antelope horns.

Fragrances range from sweet to spicy, pungent to heady and even to foul. Such diversity exists, in fact, that it is hard to list all possibilities. Orchids grow on and in nearly anything from rocks to sand, bogs to trees and fern roots. They are found in native lands all over the world from tropics to arctic areas, but the greatest variety and number come from warmer countries and are tropical flowers.

Overcoming false rumors of the past, such as: the "parasite" misnomer or "cannibalism" theory; "orchids require a hothouse;" or "orchids are fabulously expensive...only for the rich" syndromes — orchids are exploding in popularity. Prices for fine plants are within reach of any gardener today.

Orchids are not as expensive as other favorite flowers in comparison to durability and beauty extended. Many orchid blossoms last months on the plants and almost half that as cut flowers. Thus you might spend $10. for an orchid and the same for three All-American Roses but the orchid would give more blooms and stay in bloom months longer than all the roses, then the orchid plants live for your lifetime to be passed on to your children. This would make orchids' cost for decorative purposes lower than most other beauties. Orchid plants can live to be at least 125 years old; few other garden beauties can match that — therefore original cost is comparatively small when buyers understand benefits. Orchids can live on only light, air and water although most growers today transplant and feed them for best results, whether they are terrestrial or epiphytic. The majority come from subtropical and tropical countries. They are mostly epiphytes found growing on trees, shrubs and rocks at altitudes between 1,500 and 7,500 feet although some are found from sea level up to 14,000-foot-cool mountains. Most grow where there are definite dry and rainy seasons.

Like Apollo spaceships most orchids have redundant safeguards or back-up systems and replacement apparatus to rescue them from unusually bad weather conditions or inept growers — at least sympodial orchids like Cattleyas, Epidendrums and Dendrobiums are designed this complex space-safety way.

Appeals of orchids are almost exclusively intellectual and aesthetic. Except for small commercial value of vanilla extract which can now be synthetic; salep products; the olden belief of orchids' sexual potency from which the name originated; and a few perfumes; orchids appeal to humankind's higher nature. Today, orchid treasures are found as houseplants and garden favorites wherever thinking people live. Orchids seem destined to hold their revered place as Royalty of the Flowering World.

BROMELIADS — Fancy Air Plants — are exciting and "new" enough to incite a riot of current interest in horticultural/hobbyist circles as well as the formation of Bromeliad Societies. Changing tides of popularity have floated Bromeliads in and out of homes and gardens but it is "high tide" for them now. Bromeliads are extraordinarily varied and unique with their striking inflorescences, colorful bracts and graphic-designs in leaf urns and rosettes which catch the eye. Actually two Bromeliads — Pineapples and Spanish Moss — have been grown commercially for over 100 years. Indians used Spanish Moss for bedding (red mites notwithstanding) and shelter. Later settlers gathered it from trees for use as mattress stuffing and gun wadding. Overstuffed furniture and upholstery in Model "T" Fords was made of Spanish Moss well into the 1930's. A few hobbyists and botanical gardens have grown them for 40 years and at least two commercial nurseries in the U.S.A. have been selling them for about 25 years but Bromeliads have been in and out of favor within the last 10 years. Only has better knowledge helped rapid growth in popularity to make them favorite flowers today.

THE PINEAPPLE FAMILY *(Bromeliaceae)* is the same one which supplies the famous fruit and juice as well as the decorative Bromeliads. Just different family members. They range from the soft ghostly droopiness of Spanish Moss to spiny terrestrial monsters, to shapes of fiery swords, to inflorescences displaying color combinations certainly unusual to the Vegetable World if not actually close to the Orchid's World. There are more than 1,300 species and about 60 genera from the West Indies and Tropical Americas, known at this time. Within this family are some Bromeliads that are large harsh leaved, spike-studded "bull-high, hog-tight, rat-snag" guardian fences *(Bromelia blansae* and *B. pinquin)* but these are rarely grown by hobbyists. In fact, spininess repelled people as did the center "cups" that hold water in which mosquito larvae once flourished. Billbergias were fast growing but their flowers were also "fast going." Hybrids have been developed and new species imported with long-lasting inflorescences that brighten interior art of living mobiles and driftwood "Bromeliad-trees." Vriesias — soft-leaved spineless genera with glowing scarlet, tightly overlapping bracts that form "flaming swords" in many species spotlighted the "loveable" colorful inflorescence Bromeliads. They became a "rage" in the late 1940's. Modern air transportation brought more transit — perishable species, even some with pretty true flowers, such as *Tillandsia cyanea.* Miniatures such as Blushing Bride, *Tillandsia ionanthe,* that turns red all over and eventually grows into large mats of color. The more attractive foliage Bromeliads make unusual house plants but they are also striking for edging a garden, used as a ground cover or in driftwood-designed planter gardens. Bromeliads can be attached to trees, bushes and fences in warmer climates or to pieces of driftwood to decorate patios. They are simply tied where they are supposed to grow and sprinkled frequently until established if the atmosphere is dry since the small roots would be fully exposed. Many will adapt to soil too if it is porous so they may dry out between waterings. Most Bromeliads hold water in their tubular or rosette leaf forms so they can take care of their own needs.

Population explosion, servant shortages and "high-rise" sprees causing moving to smaller homes or apartments, have increased demand for smaller Bromeliads just as for smaller orchids. Because both are tough plants that can take care of themselves they vie for top position as houseplants. Bromeliads can stand even drier air, less light and can even endure a little gas in the air. Plantsmen cultivated and imported smaller, softer, miniature cupless varieties — Tillandsias mainly — and drier growing terrestrials, Hechtias and Dyckias. Some species will also grow in a north window with little or no direct sunlight, especially the tougher Neoregela, Billbergia, Cryptanthus and Nidularium types. In fact, all Bromeliads are especially adapted to survive periods of drought or neglect and dim light, but some hybrids require more light to do well. Cold tolerance has not been properly researched but these have been known to survive 18 to 20 degrees for short periods, rare for tropical flowers: "Queen Tears." *Billbergia nutans,* glittering with radiant pink bracts, flowers of metallic blue and chartreuse with conspicuous golden yellow stamens — this is the hardiest and glamourous parent of many hybrids; Fingernail Bromeliads *(Neorgelia spectabilis)* with each leaf tipped blood-red and small lavender flowers that appear in water in leaf-cup in late spring to early summer; Flaming Torch, *Billbergia pyramidalis,* with soft apple-green leaves and in winter brilliant red spikes tinged with bright blue blooms; and Heart-of-Flame *(Bromelia balansae)* so dangerously armed with vicious hooks on narrow gray leaves that arch out 3 or 4 feet, it's rarely a hobby plant, but becomes beautiful in spring when the center leaves turn red and the inflorescence shows scarlet bracts and maroon flowers; Cryptanthus — star-shaped, variegated flattened terrestrials from Brazil make a fine ground cover while C. 'It' has been a prize-winning houseplant.

Grecian Vase, *Aechmea marmorata,* has mottled leaves in stiff, recurving vase-like form. Springing from the center, a pendulous inflorescence will have pale pink bracts and blue-petaled flowers. Glamorous Grecian Vase, *A. fulgens,* grows pale green leaves in a basal rosette with numerous blue-tipped flowers with red calyxes designed on a stiff panicle that will be ornamental for a long period. Many Aechmeas are prized in cultivation but newer hybrids of this and other genera offer more for today's hobbyist.

CACTI AND SUCCULENTS — children of adversity — learned to adapt themselves to changing ages during evolution. Cacti and Succulents — such all-inclusive names for such unique beauties — offer some of the most popular and useful plants

(Continued on page 103)

Descriptions of the following pictures

Page 81

Flame Vine, Orange Trumpet, Trumpet Creeper *(Pyrostegia ignea* or *Bignonia venusta)*

Sheets of flame cover trees, fences, walls and roofs when the Flame Vine is in bloom. The long slender red-orange tubes seem to be tongues of flame sweeping over the vine almost engulfing or hiding the green leaves and tendrils. Pyrostegia is Greek for fire and roof — roofs covered with this vine do seem to be on fire. Several varieties of these are native to the Caribbean and Brazil.

Page 82

Allamanda, Golden Bell, Golden Trumpet *(Allamanda cathartica)*

Yellow Allamandas are popular vines which quickly cover fences, walls or buildings if tied up for they do not seem to cling as other vines. Because of this, they often remain as shrubs or clumps of glossy-green leaves perked up by profuse "solidified sunshine" in velvety yellow bells. Their buds are shades of chocolate and shiny — as if someone varnished each one. It is from Tropical American countries but grows easily in any warm country or greenhouse.

Page 83

Sky Vine, Blue Trumpets *(Thumbergia grandiflora)*

Large blue flaring flowers with yellow throats are striking against the deep green heart-shaped rough textured leaves and this vine from India. The leaves grow to 8 inches long while the vine is a very strong climber, producing pale to dark blue flowers abundantly. Unless trained these may be at a height where they cannot be appreciated — as much as 50 ft. — but are stunning over a pergola and it blooms nearly all year. The white variety alba does not seem to grow as robustly. A small shrub in this genus is T. affinis with dark violet flowers. It grows to 3 ft. in full sun. The Bush Clockvine, (T. erecta,) grows to 4-5 ft. and is often used as a hedge with its dark blue flowers; from Tropical Africa. From East Africa, the Black-eyed Clockvine (T. alata) is golden. A few yellow or white varieties do not have "dark eyes" but all bloom in late summer or early fall.

(Continued on page 97)

FLAME VINE

ALLAMANDA, GOLDEN TRUMPET

For detailed description see page 80

SKY VINE, THUMBERGIA $\rightarrow$

*BLUE
PASSION FLOWER*

For detailed description see page 97

PURPLE GRANADILLA

84

PASSION
FLOWERS

RED PASSION FLOWER

SCARLET PASSION FLOWER

85

BOUGAINVILLEA
SPECTABILIS: SUNGLOW →

BOUGAINVILLEA

↑ BOUGAINVILLEA GLABRA →

For detailed description see page 98

CORAL VINE, MEXICAN LOVE CHAIN

PETREA, QUEEN'S WRATH
WREATH

For detailed description see page 99

IXORA,
FLAME OF
THE WOODS

ANTHURIUM,
FLAMINGO
FLOWER

90

PELICAN FLOWER

For detailed description see page 100

SHRIMP PLANT

91

WITH BIRDS OF PARADISE

← *WITH CYMBIDIUM ORCHIDS*

TROPICAL FLOWER ARRANGEMENTS 93

QUEEN OF THE NIGHT

For detailed description see page 102

← MONSTERA DELICIOSA

PEACH ANGEL'S TRUMPET

(Continued from page 80)

Descriptions of the foregoing pictures

Page 84

Passion Flower, Blue Passion Flower, Crucifixion Story Flower *(Passiflora caerulea)*

Passion Flowers show the story of the Crucifixion in symbolism. Early explorers started the legends which continue today. First, the shades of purple have signified Christ's passion on the cross since earliest times. Purplish parts that flare into a many-pointed star always number 10-apostles at the Crucifixion (Judas and Peter absent). Centered is a sunburst blue, white and purple filaments of the corona numbering 72 which ancient tradition says were the number of thorns in the Crown of Thorns. Five anthers symbolize the five wounds. Three nails are there in the form of three styles with rounded stigmas. Cords and whips are seen in the coiling tendrils of the climbing vine; clutching hands of the persecutor-mob in the five lobed leaves. Lance-shaped leaves in some varieties symbolize spears Roman soldiers pierced into His side. Some have angel-wing leaves. Some have odd whitish spots on the underside which are likened to the 30 betrayal coins. On the back of flowers are three sepals symbolizing the Trinity. All but a few of the 300 species are native to the New World and many have edible fruits.

Page 84

Passion Flower, Purple Granadilla *(Passiflora edulis)*

This Purple Passion Flower has purple egg-shaped fruits which are edible.

Page 85

Red Passion Flower, Giant Granadilla *(Passiflora quadrangularis)*

Loveliest and most striking of all the Passion Flowers is the Red Passion Flower pictured (there is another smaller red, P. coccinea). Its most unusual feature is the crown with its purple and white-banded curly filaments which are longer than the red petals. The petals are red on both sides but the five sepals are red inside and green on the outside. Another charming feature is its fragrance. Like all of the Passion Flowers, this beauty tells the story of the Crucifixion in symbolism. Giant Granadilla fruit supplies the juice for delicate drinks, sherbets, jams and jellies — as can all edible fruit.

97

Page 85

Scarlet Passion Flower *(Passiflora coccinea)*

Striking flowers in any color, scarlet Passion Flowers are exquisitely beautiful. Passiflora is Latin for passion-flower, in allusion to the blossoms suggesting the Crucifixion.

Page 86

Bougainvillea, Colored Paper Flower *(Bougainvillea glabra)*

This incredibly showy vine is probably the most widely planted ornamental vine of the tropics and a favorite in other southern areas. The vivid magentas, purples, reds and salmons you see are not real flowers but rather, come from three bracts which surround tiny flowers. Texture of these bracts also gives them the name of "Paper Flowers." This vigorous thorny climber can be seen covering 70 foot trees or trained as hedges and shrubs. Their name comes from a French navigator, Louis de Bougainville, whose plant-hunting botanist brought specimens aboard in Rio de Janeiro in 1768 while supplies were being loaded. Bougainville was the first Frenchman to sail the Pacific on an expedition to the South Seas but his name is more remembered in this showpiece flowering vine of the tropics. It seems to bloom best in poor soil so even rocky mountain slopes and dry barren areas can support its color.

Page 87

Bougainvillea 'Sunglow' Crepe Paper Flower (*Bougainvillea spectabilis 'Sunglow')*

Most free-flowering and commonest forms are evergreen climbers. B. formosa *with clusters of deep mauve bracts with yellow flowers within, and* B. glabra *with purple to magenta bracts (used so much in hedges but can be pruned into pot plants) while* B. spectabilis *has the most varieties in colors of rosy-cerise, brick red, salmon, bright rose, orange and pink. All demand full sun to produce flowers in abundance.*

Page 88

Coral Vine, Mexican Love Chain *(Antigonon leptopus)*

A tiny pink Chain of Hearts dangles from this Coral Vine giving it another popular name. The vine is delicate in appearance but rugged and aggressive often growing over anything including other plants. Tangled clumps of ½ inch angular heart-shaped bright pink flowers bloom in profusion. Each spray ends in tiny but extremely strong curling tendrils able to climb anything. In its native Mexico, the underground tubers are used as food. In gardens, it can be depended upon to furnish colorful spots anywhere it's allowed to grow. Heart-shaped leaves are light green and coarse in texture. Some are such pale pink they appear white but most blossoms are bright pink and open from spring to fall. Volunteer seedlings pop up so readily in the frost-free areas that few people ever purchase this vine since home-owners give them away.

Page 89

Petrea, Purple Wreath, Queen's Wreath *(Petrea volubilis* and *Petrea arborea)*

Violet blue stars create dainty long cascades on either the woody vine (P. volubilis) *or the small evergreen shrub* (P. arborea) *in exactly the same beauty, thus either is called by the same picturesque names but the former is the most famous and from Tropical America. The entire genus was named for Lord Robert James Petre, a patron of botany. Petrea blooms several times a year in Spring, late Summer and early Autumn. The true flower actually looks a little like the old-fashioned violet of dark purple against the lighter lavender calyces which last much longer.*

Page 90

Ixora, Flame of the Woods, Jungle Geranium *(Ixora coccinea)*

Rocket fire-balls or dense clusters of 1¼″ pin-wheel flowers with 4-5 lobes spreading out from long tubes make the Ixora a most attractive evergreen shrub which may grow to small tree size. From the tropical East Indies but popular in the whole Tropical World, this relative of the coffee family has almost the same glossy leaves whorled below the fireball or snowball head. Leaves contrast with flowers and the berry-like fruit. Ixora is named for a Malabar deity. This is also called Ixora incarnata *while the orange-scarlet is called* I. fulgens, *the deeper red often* I. macrothyrsa. *There is also a fragrant white, a yellow and many hybrids.*

Page 90

Anthurium, Flamingo Flower, Heart Flower *(Anthurium andraeanum)*

Heart-shaped patent-leather like and brilliant red of this flower is its spathe. True flowers are tiny and crowded in the dense spike or spadix. Here, pictured in one of Martinique's rain forests, are dozens of buds — such as the tightly curled one just below the two open hearts — showing as flashes of red against the green heart-shaped leaves. The Anthurium genus is widely grown for its fine foliage or its striking flower spathe. A sister plant (A. scherzerianum) *is also called the Flamingo Flower or Pig Tail Flower.*

Although its spathe is colored like these pictured, its spadix coils like a small corkscrew and the spathe is never quite as waxy or brilliant red, orange-red (or even as white) as the one pictured here. Nor does its bloom last as long. This Anthurium flower will last for the florist as a cut-flower for three weeks when cut at its prime. It will last even longer on the plant.

Page 91

Pelican Flower *(Aristolochia grandiflora)*

This view looks into the heart of a fantastic flower which is also a cleverly designed insect trap. Before this flower opens it looks like a long-tailed Pelican; the part that is open would have appeared then as the body-part resting on water. Notice in the open flower that there's a purple path-design leading to a dark maroon section. This is actually a hole or opening leading to the trap. Insects are attracted by this area and the scent coming from it. They follow this scent along a path that curves through a tunnel or the neck of the pelican to the head. Insects do not seem to notice they are crawling over fine hairs pointing inward. They only realize this when they turn around and attempt to get out. Then they face these sharp hairs which act like barbed-wire fences keeping the insects hedged in. After the blossom has been open for awhile insects can be felt buzzing inside the "head" or their shadows can be seen if bright sunlight is behind this part of the flower. The flower does not seem to "eat" these insects it traps but rather uses this as a means of fertilizing the roots as the filled traps drop to the ground and decay. This unusual plant originated in Jamaica with its relatives spread into South America.

Page 91

Shrimp Plant *(Beloperone guttata)*

Heart shaped rosy bracts overlap each other in scale fashion forming a curve with true flowers appearing from inside the tube near the tip end. Curved bracts and flowers together look so much like the curved tail of a shrimp that even highly scientific people are more likely to call this herbaceous little shrub by its common name. (Besides, Beloperone is a Greek allusion to the arrow-shaped anthers which aren't readily seen). The Shrimp Plant is a native of Mexico but grown in many tropical gardens over the World.

Page 92

Cymbidium Orchids – Long Lasting, Lovely Arrangement Flowers *(Cymbidium sp.)*

Tall, arching sprays of large curiously shaped Cymbidium Orchids lend a modern Oriental grace to flower designs and these blooms may last from 4 weeks to 3 months. These Orchids are a genus of terrestrial or epiphytic orchids from the Far East Asian Tropics and Sun-tropical lands with about 70 wild species. Thousands of hybrids now grow in outdoor beds and commercial fields in California and Hawaii with some warmer growing miniatures now gaining in popularity in Florida and Texas. Hobbyists grow them wherever there is room or proper temperatures.

Page 93

Bird-of-Paradise Flower Arrangement *(Strelitzia reginae)*

Strikingly colorful and abstract designed flower arrangement is created featuring Bird-of-Paradise blooms, Screw Pine Pandanus geodesic globe-fruits, straw flowers and greenery including the perforated Monstera leaf. Such an arrangement is quite long lasting as well as attractive. Arrangements by Jenny Schroeder.

Page 94 and front cover

Monstera Deliciosa *(Monstera deliciosa)*

Monstera Deliciosas are also called 'Ceriman' or "Giant Jack in the Pulpit," "Delicious Monsters" and "Locust-and-Wild-Honey". About 21 species are also called "Swiss Cheese" plants. They are from Mexico and Guatemala primarily but grow in most Tropical American countries or warm areas where they have been introduced. This plant is known as Philodendron pertusum *in its juvenile stage. The Monstera Deliciosa's unique calla-like "flower" has a heavy-textured curled spathe, that is hood-like pointed, as an up-ended boat, protecting a cone-like or rocket-shaped bisexual spadix with divided young six-sided corn-like fruit sections. It takes about 14 months to ripen, and the entire fruit has a slight pineapple aroma. As the fruit ripens the fragrance is stronger. Corn-sections enlarge adding orangish-yellow color to become an edible delicious fruit tasting like a combination pineapple-apricot-mango-banana. The Monstera is a tree-climbing woody vine forming long aerial roots. When mature, its large oval leaves are glossy green to 3 ft. pinnately slashed and/or perforated with oblong holes. An exotic shade-lover, it reaches toward the sun.*

Page 95

Queen of the Night *(Selenicereus grandiflorus)*

Queen of the Night is a good name for this large flower which could be said to resemble a crown but it's usually described as a many-petaled cup. White flowers, fragrant like vanilla, bloom at night and are up to 6 or 7" in diameter with a scaly outside often with tufts of grey hair around the outer segments — salmon colored. It can be seen climbing or trailing from trees from the Caribbean area into the Bahamas, Florida and Bermuda. The fruit is berry-like but covered at first with bristles, hairs and spines. It is often confused with other night-blooming Cacti but the difference can be seen in the ribbed or angled stems with small sparse spines. It is often called Hylocereus (H. undatus, H. lemairei) *and* Cereus grandiflorus *but some of these are not fragrant. Selenicereus named for moon goddess and cereus. It is of unknown origin but has naturalized in many tropical areas.*

Page 96

Peach Angel's Trumpet *(Datura suaveolens)*

Peach-yellow or pale salmon colored trumpet flowers 10-12 inches long hang among downy-like long green leaves from a shrub 8 to 15 ft. originally from Brazil, similar D. mollis *from Ecuador. It is sweet-scented with heady musk at twilight and evening. It blooms three or four times a year. There is a white,* D. candida, *from Central America, Mexico and Baja California; a Scarlet Trumpet,* D. sanguinea, *from Peru originally but seen also in Mexico, California and Florida; and the Devil's Trumpet,* D. metel, *from India and Asia with twisted upturned petals of purple and white. The last two have been used for narcotics (seeds for poisoning). Most are said to be toxic if eaten.*

(Continued from page 79)

today for house culture plus unusuals for exterior decor, contemporary landscaping, rock gardens and wall plantings. Larger ones — in their native habitats — supply fantastic sightseeing. Like some Bromeliads, Cacti are used for "Bull-High, Hog-Tight" fences, in Mexico, for instance where Cacti is used as well for food, firewood and drinks. Certain Lobivias may never be more than one or two inches high; Giant Cactus may reach heights of 60 feet and weigh several tons.

Giant Saguaros — arms raised as if worshipping or praising skies — when silhouetted against a desert sunset excite imaginations as does the blooming spire of a Century Plant and the heady perfume of a Night-Blooming Cereus wafting across a tropical night.

Tortured scenery like a moonscape awaits viewers of desert Succulent trees like the Pachycormus elephant-tree in Baja, California, or unearthly looking Euphorbia tree in Kenya or Cucumber trees of Socrota Island in the Indian Ocean. These are oddities to observe in their native lands but all have small relatives in their groups of genera in Cacti and Succulents, that can charm hobbyists.

Inducements to collectors are many in all these groups. Two main features for houseplant hobbyists are: that most are specially adapted in nature or will adapt themselves to environment to survive under conditions of atmospheric dryness and extreme drought; many of them — especially many Cacti — remain so small even when mature that a large number of species and varieties can be grown in limited spaces. Another delight comes with the flowers — some blooms are larger than the plants they are on (up to 12″ diameter). An apartment dweller can own quite a varied collection of Cacti and Succulents with odd designs and spectacular flowers. It is good to remember what is meant by these terms for, with few exceptions, all Cacti are Succulents but all Succulents are not Cacti. Cacti, because of their floral characteristics, belong in the Cactus Family and are native only to the Western Hemisphere ranging chiefly from Canada to South America, while Succulents are found endemic to Asia, Africa, Europe as well as in the Americas.

"Succulent" or "Succulents" are identifying terms applied to plants having thick fleshy stems or leaves. They are found in uncounted genera and about 30 families of plants including Crassula, Milkweed, Amaryllis, Daisy, Euphorbia, Lily, Mesembryanthemum, Geranium, Grape, Wandering Jew, Pepper, Oxalis, Mulberry, Caltrop, Passionflower, Periwinkle, Gourd, Sesame, Thistle and Fig-marigold. Two of these families supply the most Succulents suitable for houseplants — Stonecrop Family or Crassulaceae represented by Showy Sedum, Jade Plant, Panda Plants and Houseleek; and the Fig-Marigold Family or Aizoaceae represented by Stone-Mimicry, Window and Living Stones, Ice Plants, Sand Daisies and Tiger Jaws.

Cacti — children of the sun — evolved out of adversity to hoard water in their

103

leafless stems, just as Succulents do in their fleshy leaves, but Cacti also armed themselves for defense with spines to protect them from grazing beasts. Members of this family differ greatly in kinds of spines, form, size, growth and habitat, but all are recognized by botanists by five mutual traits.

All Cacti have an areole which is that unique cushion-like structure on branches and stems plus that each areole has two buds or growing points — lower one usually producing spines, upper producing new branches or flowers. All Cacti are perennial requiring more than one season to mature but not dying after flowering as annuals do. All Cacti have wheel-design or flare-shaped flowers containing an indefinite number of petals and sepals. Also the fruit is formed below the flowers. All Cacti have fruit which is a one-celled berry and seeds are scattering within it. Some, such as the Prickly Pears, are prized food. Lastly, all Cacti seeds produce two embryo leaves when they germinate. The Cactus Family supports some 2,000 species which may be terrestrial, epiphytic or semi-epiphytic and grow in moist cloud forests or arid deserts with marvelously diverse forms. Some are barrel-like such as the Golden Barrel, geodesic globes, deeply fluted or flattened and climb like vines, columnar, cylindrical or jointed links, like sausages.

True "Beauty and the Beast" Cacti — flowers are mostly large and usually strikingly beautiful such as the Night-Blooming Cereus, Indian Strawberry, Gooseneck and Rose Cactus. They are water-misers but generous with flowers that turn into fruit. Only one genus, Pereskia, has conventional stems or leaves. Grown in the tropics as ornamentals with olive-sized yellow fruit, or variegated colored leaves or fragrant flowers.

Orchid Cacti ... Slender Torches ... Christmas Cacti ... Easter Cacti ... Sun Goddess ... Scarlet giant — Epiphyllum group of species and hybrids are the sub-tribe Cereanae — the names hint at the variety of large and beautiful flowers up to 10″ in size often on many branch plants. Seeing a collection of these in bloom explains hobbyists' zeal.

ANTHURIUMS — "Tail Plants," "Flamingo Flowers," "Painter's-Palette" or "Heart Plant" — have decorative leaves as well as unusual flowers. The *Anthurium scherzerianum* has long been a popular houseplant although not commonly offered by commercial dealers. It is known as the "long-lastingest" blooms for some last three months and put out a new inflorescence before the old one fades. Its deep red spathe is broadly ovate, and waxy with a golden yellow or coral-colored, curly spadix decorated with tiny circles of white pollen. The plant is small — usually about 10-13″ tall — and fairly compact, making an attractive potted plant. There is a form with a double spathe dotted red or white and another the reverse of that.

Anthurium Andreanum is often called the "Flamingo Flower" too but its flower spathes may be scarlet, coral, pink or even white and are showy hearts, looking as if they had been varnished. A cream, white or color spadix with true flowers stands out from the polished spathe. Spathes are large — usually 2-5 inches wide but there are "dinner plate" sizes. They are larger than *A. scherzerianum*, 3 feet high and as much across, and not considered easy to grow unless you can furnish warmth and moisture. They are spectacular, long-lasting and worth the effort of growing. Their leaves are lush green heart shapes. Seeds take up to 12 months to mature on plants and when sown can take just as long to germinate so they are usually propagated by rooted off-shoots. There are many varieties with different sized bloom spikes.

"Green Hearts" are *Anthurium crystalinum* and *A. magnificum* primarily. They have rich velvety heart shaped leaves with contrasting silvery-white veins forming a distinctive pattern that almost glows. Many other shapes and sizes exist for to date at least 100 species and natural hybrids have been found in Colombia and the other Tropical Americas. Anthuriums are glamorous members of the Aroid Family *(Araceae)* with over 1,900 species and 107 genera including such favorites as the *Monstera deliciosa* (cover picture), Alocasias, Caladiums, Diffenbachias, Callas and versatile Philodendrons.

GINGER — Flowers and Spice — belong to a family, Zingiberaceae, that boasts about 800 fragrant species and 45 genera noted for their spicy perfumes and splash of flowers borne in spikes, hanging clusters or terminal heads. Cane-like stems plus elongated leaves often make the plant clumps 6 to 20 feet tall although there is one dwarf, 16 to 18 inch high, ornamental, *Alpina sanderae,* from New Guinea, with pale green leaves edged and banded in stripes slanting from the center to the margin with pure white. The "Common Ginger" is 2 to 4 feet high with grass-like leaves and flowers in a dense spike of green with purple and yellow lip.

Pungent floral beauties like the Butterfly, Scarlet, Kahili (a cool type from high Himalaya), Yellow and Flame Gingers are of the genus Hedychium. The genus Alpinia features five favored individuals including the porcelain-textured Shell Ginger, and the red Fiery Feather. The famed Torch Ginger, *(Nicolai elatior* formerly *Phaeomeria magnifica)* grows in gigantic clumps with canes 20 feet tall and rarely grows outside of tropical or warm subtropical areas. The White Ginger can be killed to the ground in northern Florida winters, but it recovers rapidly with spikes of spicy-perfumed white blooms in the autumn again. Because of their size and requirements, Gingers are not too common outside of the tropics but conversation pieces any place. A close relative to Ginger, rare Jewel of Burma, *Curcuma roscoeana,* from Burma, also has a magnificent spike of cone-like showy bracts which come out green but gradually turn scarlet-fire-orange with lush golden lip and yellow corolla. This is houseplant size as are other 1973 introductions; Peacock Ginger *(Kaempferia roscoeana);* Yellow Pot Ginger, *(Kaempferia decora)* and yellow-lavender Summer Ginger *(Globba winitii)* also introduced in 1973 to Western Hemisphere hobbyists.

GARDEN HISTORY CAPSULED —
BOTANICAL GARDENS

Vision and determination to collect, protect and enhance or preserve natural treasures inspired certain men and women since beginnings of recorded time — if not before. They built gardens and recorded discoveries so that their children's children as well as they might benefit. These earliest civilized people planted medicinal then food gardens then gardens to nourish a person's soul with beauty and peace of mind.

Before the times of the Pharoahs, men settled beside the Nile, Tigris and Euphrates where fresh water and sunshine helped everything grow. Here, we are taught, the first garden — The Garden of Eden — was created. The Bible tells Jews and Christians about its fruits. Confucius, Lao-tse, and Buddha, founders of major religions of the Orient, taught followers to revere nature. There are records of Chinese gardens as far back as the Han Dynasty, 207 B.C.-220 A.D. No Imperial gardens from these days were preserved for custom decreed when the head of the Royal family died, his successor would not remain in the house where death had visited. There are paintings and songs of these gardens but it took 200 years and Marco Polo's visit for word to reach the outside Western World — and some doubted what they heard.

Marco Polo said the Khan imported handsome trees and explained the Khan's astrologers said, "Those who plant trees are rewarded with long life . . ." thus roads of his kingdon were tree lined. The gardens of Cathay may have influenced other Oriental cultures certainly spreading religion did. Zen Buddhism exerted tremendous influence on landscape gardening in Japan where a Zen priest laid out gardens such as 14th and 15th century Golden and Silver Pavilions at Kyoto. At the Golden Pavilion of Kinkakuji, Kyoto, a living "Pine Ship" trained bonsai tree over 407 years old can be seen today — testament to reverence and patient skill but historians are a bit vague about whether Chinese or Korean culture influenced Japan's distinctive gardens and delightful flower arrangements.

Since Egyptian gardens were pictured in tombs in paintings, sculptured relief plus carved in heiroglyphics on walls and flowering plants were written about on papyri, we know more about these (and Plant Hunters, as you've read earlier). Of course, the Pharaoh's palaces and gardens have perished and the Hanging Gardens of Babylon laid in ruin. Rebuilt by Nebuchadnezzar about 605 B.C. then destroyed again by Persians but skilled, dedicated archaeologists have "shown" us these gardens as well as those of ancient Persians, Greeks and Romans. Homer's *Odyssey* tells of regal gardens, Pliny the Elder's *Natural History* and Pliny enlightens history too with accounts of the first potted plants for the festival of Adonis when pots were moved to housetops to display beauty as well as Pliny's notes on various garden interests during the early period of the Roman Empire.

Villa gardens of Imperial Rome added marble statues, monuments, colonnades, topiaries, pools, ornate bubbling fountains and hothouses with windows made of mica where foreign plants and 12 varieties of roses were forced into bloom. Vacation villas in Pompeii and along Mediterranean shores blossomed with secluded courts and gardens. No doubt when the Romans swept north over Europe and conquered England, they spread some floral gifts of tropical flower stories and a few seeds before Goths and Vandals sacked Rome then the Roman Empire crumbled. During the Dark Ages only sparks of divine hope kept men going and only monasteries kept gardening alive in Western Europe.

Christianity and Islam, which the Arabs encouraged by sword and the Koran, were religions that spread culture and love of gardens around the Mediterranean, India and Persia for the next thousand years. Today tourists can see the most famous garden monument — the Taj Mahal — for the Emperor's Persian wife; Shalimar, garden of Kashmir; Cordoba with its fine Mosque courtyard garden; Moorish-Spanish designs of Alcazar at Seville; the summer palace of the Generalife and the magnificent Alhambra.

Italy remained the geographical crossroads of that world so the Italian Renaissance, exemplified by such gardens as Villa Medici, Villa d'Este at Tivoli, blended with the French Renaissance, shown at Versailles and Villandry. Waves of these fashions spread to England's Hampton Court — in fact, to all Royal Palaces. These gardens and ideas inspired others around the world: Fontainebleau; Salsburg's Mirabell Gardens; Peter the Great's summer palace in Leningrad; Blenheim Palace in Oxfordshire; English mansions like Chiswick, Rousham and Chatsworth House; the summer palace of Peking and the Hall of Peaceful Seas with the Chinese 12-year cycle clock; to 19th and 20th Century American industrial magnates' estates such as Vanderbilt's "Biltmore" in North Carolina, and "Breakers" in Newport; Pierre du Pont's "Longwood Gardens" in Pennsylvania, Henry Shaw's "Tower Grove" which has become St. Louis' Missouri Botanical Garden and James Deering's "Villa Vizcaya" in Miami, Florida. These are just a few of the gardens where Italian designs spread with the influence still being felt in contemporary design.

Colonial American gardens were extensions of homeland gardens of pioneers — such as English, French, Dutch or German; reflected much later. Titled — but no immensely wealthy — people immigrated to the early colonies. Gardens were mostly edibles. What few flowers were brought — like settlers — had to be strong enough to endure cold hardships plus be useful and adaptable such as Herbs, Roses, Peonies, Lilies, Poppies and Iris. It took over 100 years for this pattern to change.

Governors' Palaces, homes and plantations, such as Tryon Palace, New Bern, N. Carolina, Mount Vernon and those of Williamsburg, in the 18th century, began to reflect accumulated wealth and a few imported tropical flowers. Today, Colonial Williamsburg, restored by generosity of John D. Rockefeller, Jr. and vision of Reverend W.A.R. Goodwin, Garden Clubs and numerous townspeople, shows a living picture of 18th century homes and gardens. Orangeries were finally built at these places and some tropical plants moved in and out with the fair weather. Most of the lovely southern plantations were destroyed during the Civil War. In the North and South after that war, wealthier merchants and officials built hothouses to protect tropical flowers. Washington's Mount Vernon was restored by efforts of Ann Pamela Cunningham, a Charleston lady.

Always garden oriented, Charleston citizens in the 19th century were importing Chinese Wisteria, Roses and Poinsettias one of their own citizens — Joel Poinsett — brought from Mexico. In fact, many plant loving Americans were importing new plants from China, Africa, Central and South America. Up until World War II, large estates had glorious gardens and massive greenhouses for tropical plants. But labor shortages and taxes in America in the 20th century doomed most of those private gardens — unless they were made into Government and Foundation showcases of Botanical Gardens supported by the public. Even these, today, must be endowed by wealthy patrons and protected with work by hundreds of volunteer members to exist in a world of high priced labor.

Vision and scientific zeal caused farsighted horticulturists of many nations to build Botanical Gardens — most started with amateurs' enthusiasm and money then helped or taken over by governments.

One of the earliest founded (of still available to the public) Botanical Gardens was at the University of Leipzig in Germany in 1542. (Padua in Italy (1540) is said to have had the first botanical garden in Europe.) It was followed by the University of Heidelberg in 1593, then by Botanischer Gardens at Kiel and Hanover in 1635 and 1666. Vienna started one but abandoned it until the next century. Paris had the Jardin Botanique de l'Université de Montpellier by 1593 and its famed Jardin des Plantes by 1635.

ROYAL BOTANIC GARDENS AT KEW. England had been busy building a world-wide Empire and the finest fleet in the world but had not neglected botany and Plant Hunters either — rather the reverse, especially during the 17th, 18th and early 19th centuries. In 1759 Princess Augusta and her son George III founded the Royal Botanic Gardens at Kew on the banks of the Thames River. King George's Royal Pleasure Boat was a replica of a huge white swan which brought him and his guests up the Thames from London to Kew. George III's mother made Kew into a center for plant research. In 1841 they were taken over by the State and in 1897 Queen Victoria donated some extra park land providing that it remain in a semi-wild state, which it does today.

Kew Gardens flow over 300 acres today, most landscaped with flowers from all parts of the world and tropical warmth loving flowers being kept in 15 glasshouses, the largest of which, the Palm House, is 361 feet long with a central section 66 feet high. There is another Hothouse nearly as big, as well as numerous buildings for libraries and 92 special gardens or places of interest for the garden lovers to visit. The Royal Botanic Gardens at Kew have long been considered the finest in the world. They have played a significant part in development of horticultural interest and scientific information which they have shared with their many other State owned gardens as well as any other country's botanists. Exotic tropical flowers Kew's Plant Hunters found have oftentimes been what saved them for today's viewers.

For over 214 years the Royal Gardens at Kew have led the way, with the Royal Horticulture Society and their Wisley Gardens and Chelsea Flower Show a close contributor.

"Mecca" for plant lovers and botanists, Kew is still contributing to botanical fields . . . still considered one of the finest sources of seeds and living plants plus World's expert in identification. Few other places can show 211-year-old living trees or let visitors roam vast greenhouses, view flower gardens such as the Rose Pergola; Sun Flowers from Mexico and Aster collections which are probably the largest in the world; be shaded by 100 year old Lebanon Cedars while admiring century old Rhododendrons from India with masses of blooms bursting from ground level to over the tallest man's head — each month there is something different in bloom among over 45,000 species from all parts of the tropical world. Though a great new Palace of Plants at Belgium's Meise Gardens has now captured the title of "World's Largest Greenhouse" by covering 2½ acres and 35 halls of plants, Kew Garden's Palm House retains its "most beautiful" crown. There are other English gardens nearby with tropical and subtropical plants such as Birminghan Botanical, Compton Acres, University of Hull, Wisley, Talbot Manor, Hampton Court, Gwylly, Tresco Abbey and Johnstone in Cornwall, to mention just a few, as well as all over the Commonwealth in cooperation with Kew.

Amazing to those who live in tropical and subtropical lands, are the discoveries that there are often more exotic blooms gathered in gardens in temperate climates such as Kew; German gardens in Berlin, Munich and Frankfort; large suspension tropical house at Edinburgh, Scotland; St. Gallen in Switzerland; France's Les Cêdres with the greatest selection of Cacti and Succulents in the Old World; or Italy's latest, Villa Taranto, created by a Scot of tropicals and subtropicals; or even in North American northern gardens such as Quebec's Botanical with large greenhouses of Orchids and Succulents; the National Arboretum in Washington, D.C., with its 10 greenhouses; Missouri Botanic Gardens with its open-space "Climatron" and 25 greenhouses; California's Huntington Gardens, one of America's grandest with its

207 acres and Desert Garden near Los Angeles; the Strybing Arboretum at San Francisco's Golden Gate Park with special plants of New Zealand; Longwood Gardens, Kennet Square, Pennsylvania, with almost 4 acres under glass or Phipps Conservatory in Pittsburgh with 21 greenhouses featuring Orchids, Cacti and other rare tropicals. But a visit to any of these does enlighten and spur activity in other countries and hometowns such as Miami, Florida.

FAIRCHILD TROPICAL GARDEN, south of Miami, has volunteer members who rarely need encouragement by "out of town" comparison or other inducement to support it although South Florida has innumerable other activities to distract attention. Fairchild Tropical Garden is the largest Tropical Botanical Garden in the United States. Its Cycad collection is only topped by that of Kirstenbosch in South Africa, which has every known species. Fairchild has 83 acres featuring a Rain Forest with Orchids, Bromeliads, Ferns and other jungle plants growing naturally in the open air. The Rare Plant House with 6,625 sq. ft. is artistically designed for viewing constantly changing flowers in bloom in pots as well as valuable rare plants growing in a landscaped garden under glass. Throughout the Garden, a representative collection of superbly grown tropical plants in a setting of good design can be viewed leisurely by walking tours or by Fairchild Rambler trams offering guided tours. There are no masses of flowers planted in annual rows but rare beauties are in bloom most every month. If there is a "best time" to visit to see the most blooms, it is mid-winter to early spring. There are 12 special plant collections with the famous Palm Collection being the largest in the Western Hemisphere. Other special collections include the Cycad, Flowering Tree, Banyan, Vine, Ground Cover, Bromeliad, Philodendron, Orchid, Bahamian Plants, Mangrove and Hibiscus Collections. Added interesting features are the Moos Sunken Garden, Bailey Palm Glade, Overlook and the Garden's Lakes which usually have as many water fowl as the trees have migrant and colorful tropical birds.

THE PALM GARDEN IN FRANKFURT/MAIN, WEST GERMANY, is famous for its collections of tropical and exotic plants as well as its music-recreation park. This garden started in 1868 with 22,000 plants and today the great Palm House is one of the largest and finest in Europe, representing a tropical scene with Palms, Ferns, Bananas, and tropical flowers such as Bird-of-Paradise and Lotus. A dozen Show Houses are dedicated to one type rarity including: Aquatics; Orchids; Cactus Family; Desert Blossoms; Begonias; Bromeliaceae; Insectivores; Succulents; Tropical Rain Forest plants; Palms and a variety of other tropicals in bloom or arranged in landscapes. There are 49 acres to enjoy and special shows at various times of the year at this Stadtischer Palmgarten Frankfurt/Main. March to November are the most recommended months for visiting.

THE BERLIN-DAHLEM BOTANICAL MUSEUM, WEST GERMANY, has Directors who group greenhouse collections according to geographical, taxonomical, ecological and economic determinations with over 20,000 species. There are six geographical houses including African Succulents, South African plants, American Succulents, American Bromeliads, Australian and East Asian plants. Next are: an Araceae house; a Tropical Orchid House; a Sun-tropical Orchid house; a Tropical Fern house; one house each for dicotyledenous and monocotyledenous tropical cultivation plants; a 53 foot tall house for subtropical plants and two large annexes — one for Tree Ferns and one for flowering plants; a tropical Aquatic plant house which is dominated in four summer months by two Victoria species: and, lastly, one of the sights of Berlin, the 82 foot tall, 197 foot long Tropical Palm House with a capacity of 57,858 cubic yards. One of the greatest men of botanical history, Carl Ludwig Willdenow, was an early Director here while one of his pupils, Alexander von Humboldt, is considered one of the greatest scientists in history. Willdenow proved sexuality in plants and was the first to make special pools for cultivating water-lilies and other aquatics at Berlin-Dahlem. Today, specially prepared historical scenes help visitors see there are trees alive that could have blossomed while Egypt's pyramids were built yet may outlive current civilizations.

BOTANICAL GARDENS OF ST. GALLEN, SWITZERLAND. Switzerland has a most unusual attraction in this garden. They do not serve any botanical university institute but rather were founded by the City expressly for the education, enjoyment and recreation of all, with free admission. Unique features are the arrangements of greenhouses into showcases for; "Attractive plants of the season;" "Tropical rain forest with bog and marginal plants, Bromeliaceae, climbers;" "Cacti and other Succulents, plants from chiefly American and African dry regions;" "Tropical industrial plants;" "Tropical and subtropical Orchids and green plants;" "Tropical 'specialists' Pitcher plants, Ant plants, etc." Also unique are the "Little Treasuries" which are noteworthy plants which tend to be overlooked in the garden. These "Little Treasuries" are raised to eye level with explanatory text. Founders felt that "because no one is obligated to visit the gardens, they had to be laid out in such a way as to attract every type person." Since 1945 this garden has introduced thousands of visitors to the "beauty, individuality and mystery of plants" in these artfully designed 3½ acres of St. Gallen Gardens.

TROPICAL FLOWERS IN HOME AND GARDEN

Tropical climates, flowers, soils and plants are diverse. It is their diversity that fascinates, but often confounds beginning tropical gardeners. Certain fundamentals can be generalized and beneficial when modified in use to suit local conditions.

Gardening is a highly personal hobby requiring intimate self-knowledge — particularly when tropical flowers are desired.

Evaluation of the hobbyists' own characteristics — preferences, dedication, lifestyle, habits, requirements and hardiness — is at least as important (if strange sounding) as determining those of plants to be grown.

Juggling plants desired with time available has caused many businessmen and doctors, for instance, to choose sympodial Orchids. Plants and blooms are of the highest order giving intellectual and aesthetic pleasure yet gardening for them may be done entirely on weekends since these orchids have bulbs to supply water and nutrients needed during the week. In fact, most can be left for much longer times without damage in summer or winter so long as warmth requirements are met. Problems usually arise when the hobbyist "falls in love" with a monopodial or an Orchid requiring a greatly different altitude than the hobbyist's. Another common problem, with acquiring Orchids as well as with other plants, is lack of knowledge of space required for growth. For instance, an apartment dweller seeing a pretty blossom, buys a seedling without finding out that the plant can grow to be taller than his ceilings and wider than his planter. Almost the same problems and advantages accrue to Cacti hobbyists as Orchid hobbyists for each plant family has members that can care for themselves.

"Investigate before you invest" is a slogan of the stock market that is excellent whether talking about securities or living plant stock. Tropical plants, especially, may fool buyers who see cut flowers only or orchids in corsages and shows without seeing their plants. Many plants are used in juvenile stage by florists for dish gardens without being dwarf growing varieties. Some Philodendrons, to be specific, are adorable miniatures in youth but soon outgrow dish gardens and terrariums. They will climb up and around the room if allowed the time and warmth for they can take enough out of the air around other potted plants to live happily.

Secrets of growing tropicals? There are just two basic "secrets" to growing tropical flowers anywhere in the world. First, acquire a healthy plant. Second, give it the environment, including light, food and water, it was accustomed to in its native habitat. These followed may even make a tropical flower bloom more beautifully than in its original home. Some imported tropicals have "gone native" in a new territory and become pests.

Anyone walking through snow flurries and icy blasts to visit a north country Botanical Garden greenhouse in winter, who then steps into an equatorial rain forest with blooming orchids or a desert rock garden of Cacti blossoms, knows that native requirements were met to make a "home away from home" for the floral beauty he sees. Usually this same visitor is amazed to find that — contrary to stories he's read about collecting in debilitating humid heat of jungles — the conservatory he's visiting is actually airy and quite comfortable. This gives another clue or secret of raising tropicals in homes. Most houses and apartments are too hot and dry or stuffy in winter for tropical plants. Moisture must be added by placing pots on gravel trays filled with water that can evaporate slowly forming humidity around plants. Fresh warm air should be circulated for best results.

Cultivation of plants in homes goes back centuries to early Greek and Roman potted plants — yet people continue to make the same mistakes. Citrus fruits were certainly grown in England in the early 1600's in "orangeries" or long rooms with many windows (a former orangery at Kew is now used as a museum). Recognition of values of growing house plants increases as more people study ecology but must move to cities. They need brightness of flowers and calmness of greenery for relief from dull sameness of concrete, asphalt and plastic man-mades. Chain stores and supermarkets in U.S. recognize this mounting trend-need thus carry some supplies formerly found only at nurseries, feed stores and mail-order catalogs.

Unless one plans to grow Mushrooms or install special lights, most plants will need to be near windows where sunlight or indirect light enters a good portion of the day. Tropicals are sun-lovers. Even shade-lovers grown in the shade, have sun that filters in or "bounces" near them with indirect brightness sometime of the day. By the same token many plants require darkness to rest and should not be planted under lights that burn all night, or they will not bloom. Some Bromeliads, Ferns, Palms, and foliage plants in general will grow for long periods in poorly lighted rooms; but most house plants and all tropical flowers need at least indirect lighting positions.

Artificial light has proven successful on such flowering plants as African Violets, Orchids, Begonias, Geraniums and Bromeliads. Thus today it is possible to grow delightful gardens even in basements with a little heating and artificial light or in normally dark rooms. All plants will enjoy a summer in the yard.

However, then they will be exposed to insects and pests not bothersome inside and require watching for such invasions.

Suggestions for starting tropical flower collections — besides reading flower books and magazines — include checking with local agricultural agents, national and local plant societies, nurseries and hobbyists to learn what is already being grown successfully. This should produce a list of interesting species and hybrids. The beginner should be able to select hardier tropical varieties which interest while the more advanced gardener chooses tropicals that may require more exacting culture thus have a wider selection. Selection of something which is not being grown in that locality may interest the adventurous hobbyist who will attempt to meet any requirements to have the most unusual tropical blossom or the rarest in his locality. Fortunately there are species, hybrids and varieties to suit any personality or degree of adventurous gardening spirit. Most nurserymen — local or by catalog — will endeavor to help in selection when advised frankly of desires, the degree of skill or degree of adventure-risk a hobbyist wishes to take. Nurserymen's selections are based on experience plus the desire to gain satisfied repeating customers and promote growing of living plants for better ecology blended with greater beauty. Each year there are new varieties of seeds and plants available from leading nurseries, some of which will become future favorites. Not all the newly discovered tropical flowers imported will adapt to home culture or even growing in a new country until more is learned about their former habitats. These — when available — allow the advanced hobbyist the added thrills (or disappointments) of growing something totally different. Risks are worth it to some, especially to those excited by the unknown ... by new rarities. (No one should smuggle any plant material past inspectors when returning from foreign travels for he might endanger his entire collection as well as the nation's.)

Garden culture of tropical flowers is limited to those "summer vacations" in the back yard for houseplants or to areas where climates and/or altitudes fairly nearly duplicate original homes of plants. Most tropical beauties will grow in subtropical zones where there is no frost or frost of very short duration. Some tropicals have had selective breeding and become aclimated to temperate zones or been grafted. Tropicals with good root systems, bulbs or tuberous roots may be killed to the ground and live again, such as White Gingers do in north Florida, Texas and Gulf Coasts. Some tropicals may live most of the year in the ground and be dug up like bulbs before freezes which are long lasting and go deep into the ground. Some temperate zone gardens grow tropicals successfully this way, in cold frames or in tubs.

Gardeners fortunate enough to live in subtropical and tropical zones, naturally, have untold floral wealth to choose from among the world of tropical flowers to grow all year in their own yards.

Garden lovers of tropical flowers in the rest of the world will have to build greenhouses, visit and join Botanical Gardens, travel to the lands of the Tropics of Cancer and Capricorn or become book-loving arm-chair travelers to enjoy these floral wonders. Flower lovers do not need ultra-modern polygraphs to reveal their returns from plants.

For those who seek — and love them — tropical flowers seem eager to waft their richest fragrances, unfold their delicate designs and bloom their brightest.

ACKNOWLEDGMENTS

In preparing this book I had the valuable assistance of several experts. Jeanne Garrard took over to write the text, which I had set up only in its basic outlines. Jenny Schroeder, a graduate of the horticultural department of the University of Bonn (Germany) inspired this book with her enthusiasm for the subject and interesting information. I could take many of the pictures in Fairchild Tropical Garden and in two expert nurseries, Fantastic Garden (Bromeliads) and in Jones and Scully's Orchidglade (Orchids) all in Miami, Florida. Doubleday and Company, Publishers, especially Robert A. Smith and Lisa Drew made the publication of this book possible. My gratitude goes to all of them in sincere appreciation.

Hans W. Hannau

Other Books by **HANS W. HANNAU:**

each one containing a collection of magnificent color photographs and a dramatic
description by this well-known photographer and writer.
The five large pictorial volumes:
U.S.A. IN FULL COLOR
with 170 color pictures
BERMUDA IN FULL COLOR
with 86 color pictures
THE BAHAMA ISLANDS IN FULL COLOR
with 62 color pictures
THE CARIBBEAN ISLANDS IN FULL COLOR
with 86 color pictures
CALIFORNIA IN COLOR
with over one hundred color pictures
The Panorama Books
each one with 30 pages of color photographs
ARIZONA - ARUBA - AUSTRIA - BAD GASTEIN - BARBADOS - BERMUDA
CALIFORNIA - CALIFORNIA MISSIONS - CAPE COD - COLORADO
COSTA DEL SOL - CURAÇAO - FLORIDA - FREEPORT/LUCAYA - GEORGIA
GUADELOUPE - HAWAII - JAMAICA - LOS ANGELES - MARTINIQUE
NASSAU - NEW ORLEANS - NEW JERSEY
NEW YORK CITY - PALM BEACH - PUERTO RICO - ROMANTIC DANUBE
SAN FRANCISCO - TRINIDAD & TOBAGO - VIRGINIA - VIRGIN ISLANDS
WASHINGTON, D.C. - YOSEMITE

Other Books by **JEANNE GARRARD:**

Award winning
GROWING ORCHIDS FOR PLEASURE
157 illustrations, 15 in color;
POTTED, small cartoon-spoof book.

Other Books by **HANNAU/GARRARD:**

FAIRCHILD TROPICAL GARDEN
with 50 color pictures
The Flora Books
each with 32 pages of color photographs
FLOWERS OF THE CARIBBEAN
TROPICAL FLOWERS OF FLORIDA
FLOWERS OF THE BAHAMAS
FLOWERS OF BERMUDA

119